SUCCESS WITH
BIG TENCH

CHRIS TURNBULL

David & Charles

This book is dedicated to lovely Binsie
in the hope that there should only be
one full moon each month

British Library Cataloguing in Publication Data

Turnbull, Chris
   Success with big tench.
   I. Title
   799.1

   ISBN 0-7153-9912-8

© Chris Turnbull, Stephen Harper, Tony Miles, Barry Snape, Roger Harker,
Len Arbery and Mike Davison 1992

Printed in Great Britain
by The Bath Press
for David & Charles
Brunel House   Newton Abbot   Devon

CONTENTS

INTRODUCTION

There are tench and there are big tench; yet despite the myths which anglers like to weave around big fish, individually the only real difference between the two is that the big ones have grown bigger than the others. Providing our tackle is up to the task, big tench are not necessarily harder to catch than their smaller kindred, except for the fact that, because they are generally the product of food-rich and sparsely populated waters, the waters themselves are significantly more difficult for an angler to come to terms with. Indeed, it is often the waters which are the main challenge in big tench fishing, rather than the quarry itself.

It has therefore been my intention to investigate rather more deeply the various approaches anglers have adopted in order to overcome the multitude of difficulties and challenges presented by big tench waters. So I make no apologies if I seem to dwell overlong on overcoming location problems and the like, for without doubt these subjects are crucial to successful big tench fishing.

While I have taken my fair share of seven pound plus tench, I could have taken considerably more. There is always the option to amass huge numbers by fishing the same hotspot on the same prolific water year in and year out; indeed, many have done that and their results have been impressive. However, I have always preferred to move on and explore the new challenges of different fisheries. In the long run this has cost me many big fish, but it has also resulted in my taking 'sevens' from five different waters. I don't claim to be alone or special in this respect – others have done as much – but I do feel it has led me to a deeper appreciation and understanding of the species than I could ever have gained by restricting my efforts to a single water.

For myself, the waters which have proved successful with big tench have ranged from shallow estate lakes, to small mature gravel pits and large shallow featureless pits, to very deep pits. However, there are still environments such as meres and reservoirs, of which I have little experience as far as tench are concerned. Indeed, is there any big tench angler who has enjoyed success from the full spectrum of waters? Nevertheless, no book on this subject would be complete if it didn't cover the approaches used successfully on all types of water. I have therefore asked a number of highly successful tench anglers to contribute chapters, which should help to make this the most comprehensive book on big tench to date.

My 8lb 5oz, taken on float tactics

INTRODUCTION

A good 25½in long, weighing 9lb 15oz, and probably its first ever visit to the bank

Perhaps I should define what I mean by big. There can be little doubt that any specimen over five pounds is a good fish. Indeed, twenty years ago these were rare enough to be considered monsters; but times have changed, and it is now indisputable that in more recent years tench have grown far bigger than ever previously recorded. In 1933 the record stood at seven pounds; since then it has climbed steadily until today it stands at over twice that weight. In fact by now, thousands of fish over seven pounds must have been taken, which is no exaggeration when you consider that there are individuals who have each caught well over one hundred fish in excess of that weight.

The true merit of a specimen should be measured against the circumstances of its capture, and most especially against the form of the water from which it was caught. While many waters struggle to produce tench over five pounds, in others the average size is well above that weight and the target may be as high as nine plus. However, very few anglers ever see tench that big; they occur in only a handful of exceptional waters, and even then their weight is usually bolstered by a considerable measure of spawn. Nevertheless, spawn-free nine, ten and even eleven pound tench turn up from

INTRODUCTION

time to time – remember the Longfield eleven? So as far as I am concerned, a tench cannot really be called big until it becomes a 'seven'.

You may disagree. However, I feel seven pounds provides us with a fairly useful definition, and it is in those waters where an angler can set his stool for fish over this weight, that a more specialist approach to tenching is likely to be demanded. After all, there is a whole world of difference between the silty millpools and other prolific waters which are the traditional home of tench fishing, and the generally large and difficult venues which provide the environments required to produce fish of exceptional size.

As little as ten years ago such fish were scarce, and only a handful of waters, mostly in the south, were known to produce them. Since then, a remarkable chain of events has produced many waters capable of providing tench of this calibre, throughout many parts of England. How long this situation can continue is debatable, but at least for the time being, tenching is undoubtedly getting better all the time.

At one time, most anglers had to travel a fair distance to stand a chance of taking a 'seven', but all that is changing rapidly. As far north as the meres of Shropshire and Cheshire; across to the east, to the pits and reservoirs of Nottinghamshire and Leicestershire; down to the Broads, the estate lakes and pits of Norfolk, and south into Essex; over to the reservoirs and pits of Hertfordshire; and to Kent, the queen of tench-fishing counties: one fishery after another can be added to the list of big tench venues. This situation is echoed in parts of Surrey, in Berkshire in the pits of the Colne Valley and in the Reading area, in the pits of Oxfordshire, and the reservoirs of Northamptonshire. Although things in the South West may not seem quite so rosy, even here the reports of big tench increase year by year – and if only anglers would refrain from constantly stuffing new waters full of carp, the prospects of big tench would brighten considerably. Why, even in South Wales where anglers bemoan the lack of viable coarse fishing, I am reliably informed of at least one water which is hardly fished yet produces fish to well over nine pounds.

It is not my intention to discuss in this book the reasons behind this phenomenal situation. Whether in the long run tenching will end in feast or famine, or return to the form of the old days, no one really knows. Besides, fish population dynamics tend to be unstable so that big fish populations rise and fall anyway; so the fact that a fishery is not producing big fish today, does not mean that it won't do so in the future, or vice versa. What *is* certain is that for the time being, big tench anglers have never had it so good. So as advice I can only endorse the words of my old mate Dave Plummer: 'Get in there and dip thy bread'.

1

LOCATION
The number one question

Everyone knows that waters such as Johnsons, Tring and Sywell produce big tench, and for the price of a permit and a few gallons of petrol, they can be fished by anyone. Many specialist anglers seldom stray from these recognised big fish waters, but others prefer to find themselves some less 'pressured' fishing. It has become a well worn cliché that 'before you can catch big fish, you must first find a water which holds them'. If you don't want to fish these so-called circuit waters, there are plenty of other worthwhile fisheries throughout the country, and a pioneering spirit can discover some priceless fishing opportunities.

How should we start in our search for a water holding the stamp of fish we are after? First of all, the angling grapevine is full of clues; many will lead only to dead-ends, but they are always worth investigation. One such tip led Simon Lush and myself to a new water which produced results beyond our wildest expectations. What's more, we found ourselves on opening day almost totally alone on a vast expanse of water. So be prepared to take some risks.

Once on the hunt, what should we be looking for? There is the question of stock density: a big tench is seldom a one-off in a water, and invariably the entire population will show a high average size. A water full of two-pounders is unlikely to produce fish of twice that weight, so we will be looking for a water where the average weight is in excess of 4 or even 5lb.

Another good guide is that almost invariably, big tench waters are very rich, with a good, balanced pH level of 7.5 to 9.0. Usually the water will be clear, often gin-clear, although it may suffer periodically from algal blooms or zoo plankton explosions which may make it cloudy. As is common in all big fish waters, because fish density will be low, our water will probably be unpopular with match or pleasure anglers. Gravel pits are perhaps most likely to fit the bill, but reservoirs, estate lakes and meres can all be worth investigation.

As you would expect with a balanced ph level, many of the best waters sit on calcium-rich chalk aquifers. Johnsons and its neighbouring lakes nest under Kent's chalk downs and provide a perfect example. Waters like these are capable of supporting a large number of big tench over a long period of time. Unfortunately for us, a chalk aquifer alone does not guarantee big tench, for while some chalk-rich areas consistently produce big tench environments, others seldom do. The River Wensum

Beautiful and atmospheric, but unlikely to be the home of big tench

in Norfolk, for instance, is a rich chalk stream which runs over a huge chalk plain. However, very few of the many pits which flank the river ever produce tench over 6lb. Probably the density of the top-soil and peat along the valley has a limiting influence on the water's potential by making it more acidic.

I will not say categorically that tench don't grow big in small waters, for there will always be exceptions. *But*, all the big tench waters I know of are large – the smallest which produces fish over 7lb with any regularity is five acres, and all the others are at least twice this size. Larger, deeper waters seldom warm up as much as small waters, and this can limit successful spawning. Poor fry recruitment levels will greatly help boost the average size of the tench, especially if coupled with high predation of smaller fish and spawn by pike and eels.

Waters which are recovering from pollution may for a while allow the surviving tench to grow quickly, since there is less competition. This happened on one of the smaller Norfolk Broads, where the tench grew from a fairly mediocre size to a respectable 7lb plus.

Phosphate from a sewage works or pig farm may seep into a water, especially pits and estate lakes, and at a fairly low level may enrich it considerably – a small amount of phosphate can produce a huge mass of aquatic plant life which will greatly benefit the entire food chain. The tench, too, may well benefit and in the short term tremendous growth rates may occur. However, if the phosphate levels get too high, the water may get too rich, and then the balance can tip from plant to algae domination; it will then no longer produce the diversity of food forms which promotes rapid fish growth, and a gradual decline in growth rates is likely to occur.

Tench are said to suffer greatly from the presence of carp in a water. However, while this is undoubtedly true of the overstocked 'doubles' waters which unfortunately we see so often nowadays, in many big carp fisheries, tench seem actually to benefit from the large amount of high nutritional value baits which are thrown in.

Fred Wilton is the originator of the high nutritional value bait theory, and he is adamant that all life in a water benefits from HNV baits. He maintains that all protein fed into a water is utilised within the entire food chain, that whatever is left uneaten or is defecated by the fish is broken down by snails and suchlike, and that eventually it is made available to micro-organisms until even the aquatic plants are fertilised by it. Others, such as Jim Gibbinson, have expressed strong doubts that bait alone can make a significant difference. For myself, I am sure that, providing the water is suitable for big tench, their growth can benefit from eating good bait, and I would urge you to keep an eye on your local big carp fisheries. The carp lads are usually so uninterested in tench that news of any big ones caught may never get onto the grapevine.

The following attitude seems to have developed in recent years, that 'once you get on the right water with a good bait, success is guaranteed'. While it holds a degree of truth – especially if an angler has unlimited time at his disposal – nonetheless it is not the whole answer: if it were, we would all be consistently successful most of the time. Locating big tench waters is only the first step towards success; it is no guarantee of it. No matter how productive a water is, big fish populations are always limited. Many anglers will struggle for a result because they have failed to locate the fish in the first place. Even the best baits and rigs can only catch fish if they are cast to where the fish are residing.

Finding the right water is child's play compared to consistently locating the productive areas in it. On well known waters the productive swims will be self-evident: excessively worn and always occupied. However, little knowledge will be gained from following the crowds or in developing an 'X marks the spot' mentality depending on the few pioneering anglers who work to find their fish. Surely there is far more satisfaction to be gained from working things out for yourself? After all, true success at the end of the day cannot be measured merely in pounds and ounces.

Many anglers seem to believe that all they have to do to catch fish is chuck a bait onto a gravel bar; but however often fish patrol gravel bars, it is worth remembering that each water is different and very often a law unto itself. There are many different features which can be attractive to tench. Humps, plateaux, bars, shelves, gullies and drop-off areas may all be highly productive, as may various margins and islands. They may be enhanced by the presence of rooted weed such as milfoil and eloda, along with lilies and reedbeds. However, some of the most consistent areas I know have no more than weedbeds, so be prepared to have an open mind.

While fish may follow certain characteristic behavioural patterns on some waters, there will always be other places that defy logic. Gravel bars may well attract anglers, but they will only be attractive to a fish if they provide for some of its biological needs: food, patrolling routes, or useful spawning areas. Therefore casting to the first gravel bar you can find may offer no more chance of catching fish than casting blind.

The underwater terrain, especially in gravel pits, can be a vastly complex affair which needs to be understood as thoroughly as possible, and an angler can never spend too much time finding out about what is down there. Usually it is easy to build a picture of one or two swims, but where possible it will pay dividends to build a complete picture of the underwater landscape. By doing this, one can work out, to a degree, why fish may be in an area at any given time. Eventually it may be possible to predict where the fish are likely to be with a fair chance of accuracy. And on a big water with a low fish density, this knowledge can make all the difference between catching and blanking.

Ultimately we need to find out not just where the bars are, but also the gullies and how they relate to each other. It is also essential to locate the drop-off areas between

Big-fish man Phil Smith using a dinghy and sonar to chart his swim

deep and shallow water, and – though to a lesser degree – any lumps, bumps, troughs or minor interconnecting channels. We need to know the depths of all these features; whether the bottom is gravel, sand or silt; where the weedbeds are, the open water, and anything else which may be relevant to the fish and which might therefore help us locate them.

By far the quickest way of charting all this information is by boat, and with the use of a sonar fish finder. Quite apart from letting you know when the fish are at home, this will give you an accurate picture of the lake bed by indicating the depth of all the contours and clearly outlining any weedbeds. Some models can even show the difference between hard gravel areas and silt. Otherwise you can use a long hollow aluminium pole, providing the lake isn't too deep to probe the bottom; though it will be a long and laborious task to compile all the information. By marking off the pole into one foot lengths, an accurate measure of the depths can be made. A rake with a long handle can also help you find out what weedbeds are down there.

Obviously the best time to do all this work is during the close season, when you are less likely to upset other anglers; but whenever it is practical and especially when fishing long sessions, I also like to be able to use a dinghy and sounder to get my chosen swim mapped out precisely. More and more specialist anglers have invested in sonar equipment, and some of the better angling shops even have them for hire, which is perfect if you only use one infrequently.

Without a dinghy, plumbing by rod and line will be the only viable alternative. This is by no means ideal, especially on large waters, as it only provides an understanding of the areas which can be cast to, which makes it difficult to build a picture of the lake as a whole. There isn't a totally accurate method of plumbing by rod and line, but failing anything else it will still be worth every hour you spend at it.

The plumbing method I use is shown in Diagram 1 and is probaby well known. However, for those unfamiliar with it, here is a brief description. After casting to an area and reeling the line tight to the lead, line can be hand-fed off the spool one foot at a time until the float comes up to the surface, giving a pretty reasonable estimate of the depth. By repeating this procedure throughout each swim, a fair picture of the contours can be formed. The buoyant extension to the lead and the large ring helps prevent the rig fouling up in all but the deepest weed. As well as being time-consuming and difficult to work in weedbeds, this rig presents another major problem: while plumbing the top of gravel bars the lead has a tendency to slip down the bar on a tight line.

The system I use is to cast as far as possible out to the left of the swim. After that spot has been measured, I reel the float back down to the lead, then lift the rod to pull the rig in about twelve feet before plumbing the depth again. After repeating this process all the way back to the bank, I then recast it a little to the right and again repeat the process. After several long casts, each one a little more to the right, all the water in front of me can be charted and a pretty good idea of the lake bed will be achieved. Any areas of special interest can then be plumbed in more precise detail...

LOCATION

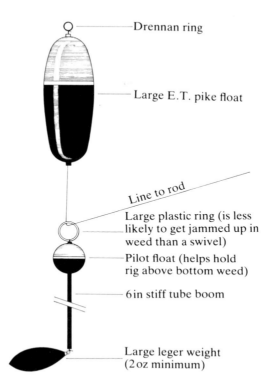

Diagram 1
Weedy water plumbing rig

Drennan ring

Large E.T. pike float

Line to rod

Large plastic ring (is less
likely to get jammed up in
weed than a swivel)

Pilot float (helps hold
rig above bottom weed)

6 in stiff tube boom

Large leger weight
(2 oz minimum)

By pulling the rig in slowly it is also possible to get a fair idea of the nature of the lake bed by feeling for resistance of the lead. If, for instance, it comes back easily with no noticeable resistance, you will be on gravel or firm sand. If there is a slightly heavy, sticky feel it is probably silt; if the lead grabs and keeps getting stuck, it is in weed; and if the line suddenly goes slack and then pulls tight you will have just pulled the lead off the top of a bar or ledge.

The importance of plumbing the depth, by whatever method, cannot be overstated; once you have compiled all the information it can only pay dividends. Several years ago I plumbed a swim to find a certain feature which I knew existed; once located, I didn't bother to explore the potential of the rest of the swim. As a consequence, I missed finding a large, seven-foot deep plateau barely forty yards out which in subsequent years became the most notable hotspot on the lake. I only caught two tench during that session – admittedly they were both 'sevens', but the following year I watched my companion, Jim Bigden, take a pile of five-, six- and seven-pounders, plus two massive beasties of 9lb 7oz and 8lb 10oz from that very plateau. Sitting in the swim next to him, I pulled my hair out at having failed to find that spot for myself when I'd had the chance.

Once all the depth contour details have been compiled, the most important task has been completed – though success is not necessarily guaranteed once we are actually

---
13

fishing. On 'pressured' waters, however, it will at least help you make the best of whatever swims are available; and should you be lucky enough to have a large proportion of a less 'pressured' water all to yourself, you will have an invaluable mine of information to work from. The chances of such a water are somewhat unlikely, but this knowledge can still work well for you. For instance, if someone is bagging up, you can analyse why the fish are in that area and perhaps choose another swim which offers the same type of environment. You would also know the exact nature of the feature he is catching off, and could possibly ambush the fish at another point as they move along it, be it a bar, drop-off or gully.

One of the most obvious ways of locating tench is visually. Luckily, tench have a habit of rolling and bubbling, especially in the morning and evening. When they are grouped up in an area, it can be stunning to watch them constantly rolling, often two or even three fish at a time. Usually this only happens at the beginning of the season, when the fish are concentrated on the spawning grounds. If ever you are lucky enough to come across such a situation, make the most of it – you could enjoy the kind of tench fishing of which dreams are made.

Tench seem to roll in two sigificantly different ways: one I call 'porpoising'. This is when, virtually silently and almost in slow motion, they lift gently from the water – first the head is visible, followed by the back and then, as the head drops back below the surface, the tail comes out. Generally I associate this movement with travelling fish; it is possible they may stop to feed on your bait, but very often they don't, and countless times I have watched them roll in this fashion over my baited swim without ever getting their heads down to feed.

When actually feeding in an area, tench often roll in a far noisier and more excited manner. In many of the larger waters they are a very mobile species, and are far from being the lazy, sluggish bottom-dwellers of popular fiction. Often they swim well above the bottom weed rather than in or under it, and when on the move they often swim in midwater or even in the surface layers – I have watched them many times as they enter the baited area. Very often they will circle the area a few times before diving down for a closer inspection, and as they do this, it is not unusual for them to turn on the surface, their flanks and tails crashing noisily as they go down. When this happens, almost invariably they will feed so it is a good time to get excited yourself.

Since the porpoising type of roll is often typical of travellers rather than feeding tench, their presence in a swim is no guarantee of feeding activity (unless you are actually catching them). And if bites are not forthcoming, it is often worth trying to work out where they are travelling to, as this may be a more productive feeding area. The knowledge gained by plumbing may give a few pointers here. If they are travelling along a feature, they may show at various different points along it. However, if they show regularly in the same spot, it is likely they are merely breaking surface as they swim over the top of a bar or weedbed.

My point is this: you can waste a lot of time fishing for travelling tench which are not prepared to feed where your bait is, when not too far away there could well be an area where they *will* get their heads down (possibly even crashing noisily at the same time). So do keep a watch out.

Bubbles are a much more easily interpreted sign of feeding fish. In older pits and most estate lakes, a lot of silt accumulates on the lake bed. These areas often hold a plentiful supply of bloodworm and other food items which may well need rooting out, and the resulting disturbance releases the gases which build up within the silt, and is a sure pointer to feeding fish. The problem is that carp, bream, eels and tench all root in silt and consequently all send up bubbles, and it is not always easy to differentiate between them. Rather than go through elaborate descriptions of each, I would describe tench bubbles as bursts of bubbles, followed by a quantity of fizzing.

There are problems with relying on bubbles to give away location. One is that when tench are feeding on gravel, they don't send them up at all. On the other hand, some lake beds bubble anyway, and really silty lakes can release so many gas bubbles that it is virtually impossible to tell if *any* are being caused by tench.

In big waters, the wind can have a marked influence on fish movements, though tench do not seem to travel on the wind to any great extent. Having said that, I have seen them do so when it was blowing a real gale. At such times it could be worth fishing the windward bank; though personally I would prefer to stay put in a swim which I knew to be regularly productive rather than chase the wind about. However, only a fool sits biteless with the wind at his back, when the tench are rolling continually on the far side of the lake.

As you get to know a water, the pattern of fish movements should begin to fall into place. In most waters there will be areas which become more productive at certain times of the year – early season tench, for instance, can usually be located on or very near to their spawning grounds. On estate lakes and reservoirs these are most likely to be on the shallow weedy areas, which are invariably near the feeder stream.

Tench usually spawn in the same spots each year, and will gather there for a good while before spawning commences; they will probably remain in the area for some time after spawning is completed, too. Generally these places are located against marginal reedbeds; on some pits the old washings bank is most suitable.

In some pits, the levels are kept low for a few years while water is pumped out of neighbouring quarries which are still being worked. When these low water conditions occur, scrub willows will grow on exposed gravel bars. However, once the pumping stops and the water table returns to its former level, the lower branches of these willows will become submerged. Large clumps of fine red filamentous root systems will then sprout from the submerged branches, and these provide a superb spawning area for tench.

It is worth paying regular pre-season visits to your waters. As already mentioned, groups of tench are likely to patrol the spawning grounds a few weeks before the season starts, and a few early morning visits may reveal the likely areas to plan fishing or perhaps start pre-baiting. Also, should the fish come in close enough, you will get a good idea of their potential size. Be careful with your estimations though, as tench have a habit of looking considerably smaller in the water. Some deeper pits may not provide any shallow spawning areas, so the tench will be forced to use whatever weed or reedbeds are available in the margins. In this situation they may be seen patrolling some of the marginal areas for many days at a time.

Once spawning is completed, tench are likely to spread out and take up residence in deeper water. Because they are most easily caught early in the season from their spawning areas, they have acquired the reputation of being primarily a shallow water species. However, do not let this blind you to other possibilities, as tench will in fact feed happily in very deep water, even in June when they should be on the spawning grounds! I well remember a tremendously successful opening week on a very distinctive gravel bar. Naturally I decided to fish the same spot during the second week, but this time without a single bite. In the end, out of desperation, I chucked a stringer of boilies ninety yards out into seventeen feet of water – within an hour it was taken by a beautiful 8lb 14oz fish, carrying a fair amount of spawn but obviously far from ready to shed it.

To make this problem of locating tench somewhat easier, an understanding of their biological requirements and basic life-style can help enormously. Food availability, weather conditions and light values all have a part to play in their movements, and they will respond in certain ways to each of these factors. As an example, many years ago Gordon Chell described in a magazine article how tench would feed at different depths down the marginal shelf according to the changes in light values. His hypothesis was that because they are sensitive to sunlight and basically dislike it, the stronger the sunlight becomes, the deeper down the shelf they would feed.

There are, of course, many exceptions to the rule and I have even seen the occasional tench basking in the margins. However, this is rather unusual and my own experiences strongly support Gordon's conclusions. Moreover, I have explored the possibilities a little further and have discovered that during the night, shortly after dawn and around dusk, tench often feed happily in very shallow water indeed, especially in calm, humid conditions. However, when light intensity strengthens, they may seem less keen to feed – if you keep your baits in these shallow areas, they are unlikely to get taken until dusk or darkness falls.

What I believe happens is that the tench move off into deeper water where they may well carry on feeding; and experiments along these lines have been fairly conclusive. For example, I spent one warm, muggy night on one of the Wensum Valley pits which holds a few big tench; my chosen swim was on the top of a large shallow hump, the sides of which sloped gently off into deep water. Both rods were baited and cast to the top of the hump, just in front of a dense bed of milfoil.

Shortly before dark, tench started rolling over the baited area, whereas previously they had only been rolling over deeper water. This pit, like most pits, seldom produced many tench at night, though by dawn I had taken a few fish. Overnight a dense mist had settled and it grew thicker as the sun rose. Bites continued for a

Jim Bigden with an 8lb 13oz, one of six 8s and three 9s he took during a ten-day session

couple of hours after the dawn, until the sun crept up over the mist, when gradually they ceased.

To the right, the hump gradually dropped off into deeper water, where a twelve-feet deep channel separated it from a series of weedy gravel bars. Leaving the left-hand bait on top of the hump, I began to experiment by casting the right-hand bait mid-way down the side of the drop-off. Before long I was picking up fish again, until an hour or two later bites dried up once more. However, by repositioning the bait even further down the drop-off I managed to relocate fish, while the bait on top of the hump still failed to arouse any interest. Eventually the right-hand bait was positioned right down in the deep channel where it produced a five- and a six-pounder, the best fish of the session, both taken in bright conditions long after the mist had cleared.

On its own this experiment would be far from conclusive, but other similar experiments have worked often enough to prove useful. Diagram 2 shows a simplified map of this pit and some observations regarding fish movements in relation to light conditions.

As a bonus from this experiment, I eventually took my best fish from the water weighing 7lb 7oz; it picked up the bait in the early afternoon on a sunny but choppy day from the deepest, siltiest trough in the lake. Another area which is often productive well into the day is the deep water at the bottom of gravel bars which have lots

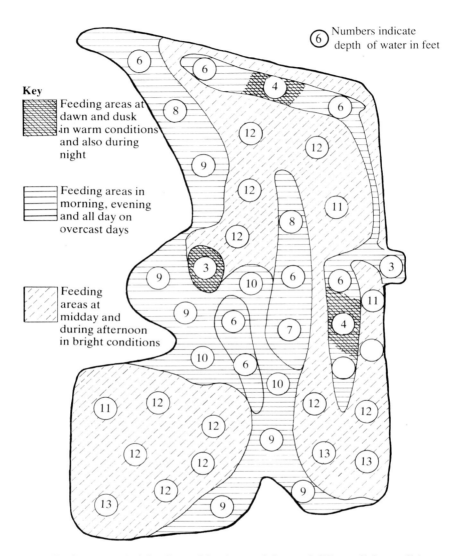

Diagram 2 Feeding areas in lake dictated by time and day and different light conditions

of weed growing down the side. It would seem that the tench often lie up under these weedbeds out of bright sunlight.

Some of the points I have raised may seem to conflict with your own experiences; however, there are no absolute truths in angling – each water tends to be a law unto itself, and tench will develop different modes of behaviour in each. All we can really do is get to know the waters we fish as well as possible, and then by constant investigation, slowly unravel the problems they present us.

2

MODERN TACKLE DEVELOPMENTS

Fishing alongside anglers on a variety of waters reveals clearly that tackle is essentially a personal issue. Therefore, any chapter on fishing tackle can also be little more than a personal view.

Over the last fifteen years, tackle has undergone an enormous revolution. Only ten years ago, the first carbon rods were just beginning to establish a market, and Optonics were a remarkable technological breakthrough. In the nineties we are now spoiled for choice, the market saturated with specialist items to the point where it is almost impossible to keep up with the never-ending stream of developments: no sooner have we paid for a product than a new one supersedes it.

Unfortunately ours is an age of hard sell consumerism, and advertisers constantly bombard us with images to make us believe that success – whether with sexy women, in social standing and now even in catching big fish – is related to how much we spend.

In reality of course, success with big fish cannot be bought. No matter how much we spend on our gear, it is angling ability which consistently puts the fish on the bank, and that has precious little to do with looking the part.

RODS

My own tench fishing has demanded a wide range of different rods. The most used and abused are a pair of two-piece, 12ft, 1¼lb test, carbon/arimids from Tri-cast. These blanks are rated with what I feel is a vastly underestimated test curve, and yet they are ideal for the weedy waters in which I do 90 per cent of my tench fishing. Coupled with 8lb line their powerful, fairly progressive action allows me to pile on the pressure when needed, but isn't so harsh that the fight cannot be enjoyed in more open water. They will lob out heavy feeders, bolt rigs or stringers up to 80 yards or more, and that's a lot to ask from any tench rod.

When I can get away with less heavy tackle and lighter lines of between 3 and 5lb, I use a pair of three-piece, 12ft, 1lb test Avons, also from Tri-cast. Although quite delicate, they still have a surprising amount of power in the middle section, all combined with a light but steely feel. The action is sweet and fairly progressive, and

An 8lb 1oz which I took from a neglected water

never seems to lock up solid under pressure. These rods allow tench to be played but not bullied, so I only use them in open water. They are perfect for close work and lighter legering, but at the same time will happily punch out a medium-sized feeder with spot-on accuracy.

These I believe were the best tench rods on the market. However, Tri-cast have unfortunately decided to discontinue their range of specialist rods under 1¾lb test curve, so unless you can pick these up as old stock or second-hand, my advice is wasted.

Nonetheless there are some super alternatives available. The 12ft 1¼lb test Specialist by Peter Drennan, for instance, seems to have power enough to do most of the things I ask of my 1¼lb Tri-casts. Also Diawa, Sportex and Conoflex produce some very nice rods in both 1¼ and 1lb test.

Anglers looking for a more all-round rod offering a compromise between those two extremes, might consider the 12ft 1¼lb test carbon/Kevlar rods produced by North Western. This blank has a lighter, softer action than the 1¼lb Tri-cast and is probably spot-on its stated test curve. In fact the action is so soft as to feel almost sloppy, which is quite unusual for a carbon rod – when you pull one around, its action seems to go on forever. It may perhaps lack the backbone for very heavy work, but must be one of the best 'all-round' tench rods available.

Not many anglers ever use a float for big tench, though a few will give it a go when the opportunity arises; and some will actually buy a custom-built rod. Until recently they had either to strain the guts out of a match rod, or make do with a 12ft specimen rod.

Luckily both Peter Drennan and Graham Phillips have come to their rescue. I field-tested one of the Drennan tench float rods and was greatly impressed. At 12ft 9ins it is a little shorter than most modern float rods, but Peter's explanation is that a rod with the muscle to deal with tench needs lots of power in its middle section. He also maintains it is impossible to build a rod longer than this which will combine sensitivity and strength without making it top-heavy in the process. I can only add that this rod feels right for the job.

Sooner or later on most big tench waters the weed growth gets totally out of hand and line strength will need to go up accordingly. Two-pound test carp rods may sound ridiculous for tench, but once a hooked fish is sulking in the middle of a weedbed, 11lb b.s. line is the lightest you can hope to use. Obviously there is little point in overworking a tench rod, so when it comes to this sort of situation, carp rods offer the only real option.

I have recommended 12ft rods because I like them best. However, where there are overhanging trees in the swim they can be a problem, and 11ft rods would be better.

REELS

Reels have seen a phenomenal rate of development, a rate of change so rapid, in fact, that it has engendered strong competition; any companies failing to keep abreast of these advances could well find their days are numbered.

For me, fixed spools are the only practical reel to use, and I keep two sets of reels to cover all my tench fishing requirements. The smaller ABU 54 reels are used for all my float fishing, light legering and most feeder-fishing work, and have taken up permanent residence on my 1lb test rods. The larger, more hi-tech Shimanos are used for all the long-range work, for bullying situations and heavy legering, and are therefore combined with the more beefy rods.

Despite all the advances made over the last decade, I cannot fault the old ABU Cardinals which combine superb solid engineering with lasting performance. Unfortunately they are no longer in production, but change hands at rather high prices on the second-hand market.

The company which has totally dominated the reel market in recent years is Shimano; the advances they have made in design are remarkable, and most of the Shimano products are quite simply hi-tech masterpieces which have deservedly acquired tremendous popularity. I doubt there are better reels on the market, though perhaps the engineering isn't quite as tough and long-lasting as it might be.

When it comes to using self-hooking rigs, until quite recently we could either fish open bail arm style or let the handle churn, and 99 per cent of the time experienced no problems. Just occasionally however, when snapping the bail arm over, the line would catch behind it; and churners can overrun, causing the line to catch up behind the flyer or bail arm. Shimano overcame this problem with their Baitrunner reels, designed to allow a run to take line freely from the spool while the bail arm remained closed.

I might not have bought my Baitrunners for tench fishing alone, but as I had been using the Baitrunner Triton Sea Spin 3500 for trolling for pike, it was inevitable they would get pressed into service for heavy legering.

At 15oz I felt at first that these reels were a little bulky when fixed onto my tench rods, but I soon got used to that. My only complaint was that line-lay on the spool was not too good and tended to encourage line-trap during long-range casting. Shimano, however, came to terms with this by producing the Baitrunner Aero Series, which incorporated their Aero line-lay spool system, combining it with a Baitrunner facility.

Shimano gave me a Baitrunner Aero GT3500 to field test and up to now I am totally impressed. My only criticism is its very large size: if its superb features could be incorporated in a reel of slightly smaller size, it would be the perfect tench reel.

LINES

Hooks and lines really ought to head the list in a chapter on tackle; rods and reels can be compromised in all sorts of ways, but hooks and lines are the main link and the one we depend on most.

Sylcast and Maxima are lines which over the years have stood out as the best. Sylcast is cheap, tough and totally reliable. It may be a little stiffer than most lines, but this seems to make it tougher and more resistant to abrasion on gravel bars and weedbeds. Some anglers are put off by its springy nature, but this need not be a problem if it is used in conjunction with braided hooklinks.

Tench tend to find their way into weedbeds during the fight and are usually there to stay – only occasionally can they be persuaded to swim out. The best strategy is either to stop them in the first place – which isn't easy, as they often get in within seconds of setting the hook – or otherwise to be prepared to drag them out, weedbed and all.

I always try a period of allowing slack line in the hope that the fish may swim out. More often than not, however, the fight ends up with the angler walking backwards with a pointed rod until something gives. This usually results in reeling in a huge pile of weed with the fish slumbering in the middle of it, for once their eyes are covered tench tend to give up altogether.

It is said that pulling fish out of weedbeds does them no harm, and many anglers maintain that when you pull them out, you are pulling against the lead and not the hook. This can certainly be the case, but there is nonetheless little doubt in my mind that pulling them out *can* damage their mouths. Big tench in weedy waters quite often bear ghastly signs of hook damage, while those in less weedy environments seldom do. Also, I have noticed that a disproportionate number seem to drop off within seconds of being dragged out of weed, which is surely evidence that the hookhold has slipped and torn free.

In my opinion this is not good angling practice, so I try to avoid fishing areas where fish are likely to weed up constantly. Few swims, however, will be totally weed-free, and those which are may well prove to be tench-free as well. There is, therefore, no complete answer to this problem, though sensible tackle and a responsible attitude will go some way towards sorting it out. This is where spools of Sylcast in line strengths of 8 and 11lb b.s. come into play; it is also when the majority of anglers shake their heads in disbelief that anyone should use such ungainly tackle.

Yet in my waters, to use anything less than 8lb test would be pointless: I go fishing to catch fish, not to lose them in every sanctuary they can get their heads into, and 8lb test is generally the minimum requirement. I try to avoid fishing swims which require 11lb line, but once the weed is in full bloom, there may be no alternative.

Where weed growth poses no problem, lighter lines can be enjoyed without fear of losing fish. With big tench I very rarely use main lines lighter than 5lb test, although hooklinks can occasionally go as low as 3lb. For this style of fishing I generally use Maxima, simply because it is more supple than Sylcast. As far as the main line is concerned, I doubt whether this offers any real advantage. However, as I usually use these lighter strains straight through to the hook, their suppleness will allow a slightly more natural presentation of the bait.

A number of double strength and pre-stretched, ultra-fine lines are available on the market, and undoubtedly these make excellent material for hooklinks. However, they are not as tough as standard monofil; they seem to lack durability and are therefore easily damaged. With the ever-present problem of losing fish in weedbeds, maximum resilience is essential and I am therefore seldom prepared to use them.

BRAIDED LINES AND MULTI-STRANDS

With many carp fishing methods now being adopted into tench fishing, it was inevitable that braided lines would find their way onto our rigs. Their advantage is obvious: whereas monofil, no matter how soft, tends to be springy and is therefore quite unlike anything naturally found underwater, braided lines are far more supple and resemble many aquatic things such as filamentous algae or fronds of pondweed; they are therefore less likely to arouse suspicion. Furthermore, as it is softer, tench

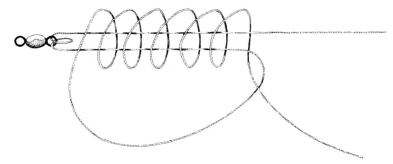

Diagram 3 Twice through the eye grinner knot

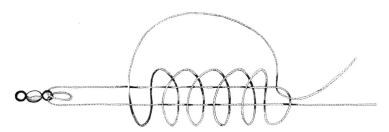

Diagram 4 Twice through the eye clinch knot

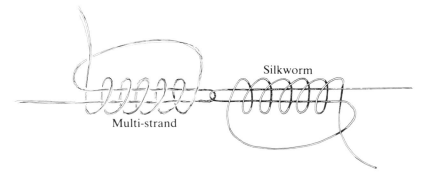

Diagram 5 Pair of five-turn grinner knots to join braided HPPE line to multi-strand

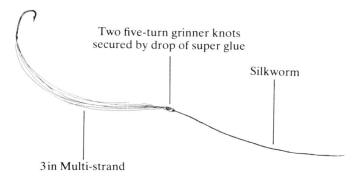

Diagram 6 Silkworm, multi-strand combination hooklink

are less likely to feel braided line on their lips; and it also allows the bait to act more naturally when sucked at.

No sooner had braided lines caught on, than every tackle company was marketing yet another new and supposedly superior brand. Most were reliable enough, but they all shared the problem of being impossible to knot soundly, making a knot which strangled and cut into itself thus drastically reducing its strength. Some knots were worse than others, and while one worked well enough with one brand it was useless with another. So while I used braids, and in practice seldom had problems with the knot actually breaking, there were always nagging doubts in the back of my mind.

Then a revolutionary new product called Kryston Multi-Strand came onto the market. The beauty of Multi-Strand is that in the water it opens out into a mist of ultra-fine filaments, making its presentation advantages beyond comparison with previous products. In practice, however, it regularly created impossible tangles. It had to be a winner, but how could we incorporate it? If the carp lads thought they had problems, they should have tried working with the long hooklinks we were using for tench fishing.

Then Kryston launched another product called Silkworm, which was constructed from Multi-Strand filaments but delicately woven together by a very fine soft thread. The result was a superbly strong, fine, lightweight and totally limp hooklink material. Even though originally its breaking strain was far in excess of anything required for tench, it was still finer and softer than the braids hitherto available and, even more important, it would tie a knot that could be totally relied on.

After successfully putting 15lb test Silkworm through its paces with carp to over 20lb, from a swim alongside of an entire oak tree blown in by the big hurricane of 1987, I was sold on it, and when Kryston released it in 8lb b.s. spools, I was really excited! There were some initial problems with the original batches which have been sorted out, and to date I consider this product to be the best lightweight braid available for tench fishing.

All Kryston products come with a recommendation that they should be tied with a grinner knot (Diagram 3), and recommend that for best results the line should be passed twice through the eye of the hook or swivel. I followed Jim Gibbinson's advice and experimented with a twice-through-the-eye clinch knot (Diagram 4); this has repeatedly proved to be superior and breaks at least at the stated breaking strain. Just to be safe I add the tiniest spot of super-glue to the knot, but take care not to splash on too much, as it will be drawn into the first $1/2$in or so of the braid and stiffen it.

So at long last tench anglers have an ultra-fine braid in which they can be totally confident, available in both 8 and 12lb spools, so covering any tench-fishing situation where a braid offers an advantage.

Thus Silkworm seemed to have superseded Multi-Strand, at least as far as I was concerned – until Kryston produced another clever idea: 'No Tangle', the anti-tangle solution, a tacky liquid compound which you rub on to Multi-Strand links. It will stick the filaments together and considerably stiffen the link, which eliminates any chance of tangling during casting; but once on the lake bed, the compound completely dissolves within a minute, allowing the Multi-Strand filaments to open out again.

So far, my experiments with this compound are limited, but the results are remarkable. My braided rigs were good, but with long lightweight braids great care still had to be taken to avoid the occasional tangle occurring, especially when feathering down the descent of the lead before entry into the water. Now I am pleased to say a blob of 'No Tangle' solution completely solves the problem.

For Multi-Strands, however, this is not the complete answer. 'No Tangle' will sort out any tangles during casting, but once it has dissolved in the water, small fish can spend hours picking at the bait and knocking it around, until eventually they turn the link into a complete mess. So what is the answer?

The real advantage of Multi-Strand lies in the last few inches of the hooklink, the bit which will touch the fish's lips. Anything else is surplus to requirements and quite honestly can only create more problems than it solves. In his column in the *Angler's Mail*, Andy Little suggested unravelling the last few inches of Silkworm and removing the thread which binds it together, so that the filaments next to the hook could open up. This is a rather fiddly operation, but I found that it was no problem to tie a short length of Multi-Strand onto the end of a longer length of Silkworm. I do this using a pair of five-turn grinner knots (Diagram 5), then a spot of super glue to bond them.

The result (Diagram 6) is the ultimate hooklink, and the only possible way of improving on it is to tease out and remove about a third of the Multi-Strand fibres beforehand which will reduce it to approximately 10lb b.s.

HOOKS

There are so many hooks on the market that it would take a lifetime to compile their various merits. I like a hook to be as light as possible for delicate presentation, and forged for strength. It should be needle-sharp, and micro-barbed so that it can be removed causing minimum damage to the fish's lips.

The Drennan Specialist and Super Specialist chemically sharpened hooks adequately incorporate all these features. The Specialist hook is finer in the wire and almost lethally sharp, and some anglers say that it is so fine, it can cut its way out of the hookhold. This may be true with big carp, but I cannot say I have noticed it happen regularly with tench, unless possibly when they get weeded up. I use them unreservedly for all my lighter fishing, coupled with lines up to 8lb. When using lines above 8lb b.s. I use the Super Specialist hooks, and these have done everything I could reasonably expect of them.

Tench have very tough lips and once a hook is set in them, it usually gets a good hold. Inside the mouth, however, the tissue is very soft and tears easily, and small hooks can therefore do horrible damage by causing long gashes as the hookhold slips. To prevent this happening, I try to avoid using hooks smaller than size 12, unless fishing in open water with fine lines and balanced tackle; then it is possible to coax a big fish in gently, without pulling hard on the mouth tissue. However, in most of my waters no such luxury can be afforded.

While on the subject of chemically etched hooks, it pays to check them regularly as the points have a tendency to bend over should they get bounced across gravel bars while reeling in.

BUZZERS

For many years I have been using Optonics for all stillwater legering. Currently I use the Super Compacts, preferring the four-vaned wheels because they offer more sensitivity. Should small bites be a big problem, both Kevin Nash and Ivel Trading Co market special 'Twitcher Wheels'. These fit into an Optonic and give the buzzer such great sensitivity that it will squeak even if a shrimp sneezes on your bait.

More recently the manufacturers Sundridge have improved their range, and brought out the Super XL Optonic which incorporates all the features of the now deleted Delkim modifications. Without doubt these will become the most popular of the range.

Last year I was asked to field-test a pair of Bitech Vipers complete with an extension sounder box. The design of this product is superb, especially the LED lights which stand above the rods and are therefore easily visible from all angles. With lines above 8lb test and using heavy bobbins or monkey climbers, these buzzers proved superbly sensitive. However, they fail to deal effectively with light lines and light bobbins, and this only makes them suitable for use with self-hooking rigs.

The Bitech extension box, however, is without doubt the best of its kind. Designed to work with all 2.5mm jack plug systems, it is also suitable for use with Optonics. It will connect to three rods and incorporates tone and volume controls, a red flashing run LED, and has three different colour latching lights to tell you which rod is away. In the bivvie, I can now have the volume set loud enough to waken the dead, while outside the buzzers are turned low so that they will not disturb other anglers.

ACCESSORIES AND SUNDRIES

To avoid being tedious, I will try to keep this section as short as possible and will assume that most people know that artillery forceps remove hooks, that Drennan and Berkley make the best swivels, that high factor sun-cream prevents sun-burn, and that you can't stalk tench if you can't see them so a pair of Polaroids helps. Now let's move on.

The majority of big tench waters are gravel pits and most of these have banks as hard as iron, so you can waste a lot of time hammering in rod rests. Cheaper ones cannot take the strain for more than a few visits, and even stainless steel buckles eventually – therefore buy the strongest you can.

I must confess to having an irrational dislike of rod pods, but nonetheless the fewer banksticks and monkey needles you have to hammer away at, the easier life will be. Also, your approach will be a lot quieter and there is much to be said for not spooking the fish before you actually get your baits out!

In an attempt to get the best out of my tench fishing, my efforts are often spent a long way from home on waters which offer the sort of potential not available locally. And when bivvied up for a few days or more, comfort becomes an issue of great importance – I am no longer prepared to slum it for my fish! In June the days are long and can get stiflingly hot, while nights are short, offering less chance to get some rest; and even in midsummer they can get very damp and cold. In order to make the most of these sessions it is important not to lose enthusiasm through tiredness due to lack of comfort. After all, fishing is supposed to be enjoyable, not an endurance test.

A good bivvie is therefore invaluable. Mine consists of a 50in Steadfast Nubrolli, combined with a 50in Kevin Nash canvas overwrap, and fitting groundsheet. This combination provides a warm, dry and stable shelter, in which the umbrella pole is completely removed to provide maximum room. There are lighter, more convenient bivvies, but none can match the comfort that canvas affords. At night they are warm and – being of 'breathable' stuff – do not trap condensation; during the day they do not produce anywhere near the sizzling temperatures of nylon bivvies. They are also more stable in high winds and will not keep you awake all night with endless flapping.

The next most important thing is the bedchair. A sun-bed is all very well, but the Fox International Super Delux Adjusta-level Bedchair, though not cheap, will make the experience of camping out far more enjoyable. Its legs adjust for stability on unlevel ground, and its sprung, foam-filled mattress ensures a high degree of warmth and comfort.

During long sessions when there may be bait to prepare as well as meals, a camping gas stove with double burners takes a lot of beating, but for shorter stays, a Peak 1 Feather 400 stove is unbeatable. One fill-up of fuel provides a full-power burning time of 1hr 15min and it will simmer for up to $2\frac{1}{2}$ hours; even in mid-winter, it will boil a kettle in minutes. And when you have finished with it, being lightweight and compact, it will fit neatly into your holdall. Many anglers burn lead-free petrol on three stoves, but you get a cleaner, longer-lasting performance if you use Coleman fuel.

Simon Lush draws a biggie to the net

One word of warning: to cook inside the bivvie is to court great danger; in an accident the bivvie goes up in flames unbelievably quickly. It happened to me once, and I was lucky to be outside when it blew, otherwise I would have suffered major burns. If you ever go to Kent and hear of an angler called Chris Fireball, you now know who they are talking about!

Your kit is not complete without a 36in bow-framed landing net. Also a 6ft handle is an advantage where there is marginal weed.

Take a number of standard-sized, soft nylon carp sacks. I never use keepnets, and dislike them intensely as they cause unnecessary stress and damage to fish. Tench should be kept one per sack, sunk out of direct sunlight, for as short a time as possible.

Last of all is a soft sling or weigh bag. Always dampen it before weighing a fish, and zero the scales with the sling hanging from the hook. Dial scales like Avons can only be zeroed accurately under tension. If your procedure is right and providing your scales are regularly checked, you should get the true weight every time. It's worth the effort to weigh fish properly; after all, what's the point of having a true 8lb 14oz recorded at over 9lb or for that matter at less than its proper weight?

3

FLOAT FISHING

It is, perhaps, a sad reflection of this modern hi-tech age that float fishing is a technique hardly used now by big tench specialists because of the advances made by electric bite alarms and legering techniques. Personally I would hate to have to return to many of the limitations we lived with in the past, and acknowledge how much we owe to these remarkable developments, but let us not forget that time-honoured methods can still have their place and at times cannot be bettered.

Many specialist anglers, especially those in the carp scene, come into angling without ever gaining the experience of a long, hard-earned apprenticeship which would guide them through the diversity of methods and species. Few of them, therefore, will ever experience the fascination and anticipation of watching a well cocked float while it knocks and dithers in response to line bites amidst a profusion of glittering tench bubbles. This is a beautiful way of catching tench. True, it will not be suited to all waters or all occasions, but nevertheless, when practical, float fishing is unbeatable as the most sensitive and efficient method of presenting a bait we have at our disposal.

Any successful match angler will tell you that a float will respond positively to bites which even the most sensitive of legering systems barely shows. Try legering in stillwaters for small roach, for example: each time you reel in, your maggots will have been sucked to shreds – and yet you would be lucky if you saw even a few tiny knocks. We all know that when legering, tench can pull so hard that the bobbin crashes into the butt ring and the reel handle churns to a blur. The fact is, however, that these are rarely the antics of confidently feeding tench, but rather a terrified reaction as they bolt out of the swim, panic-stricken by the resistance of the rig.

Watch tench feeding close in, in clear water, and you will realise how delicately they can feed, even when crowding to mop up a mass of tiny particle baits. In this situation, even the most sensitive legering rigs may have severe limitations in registering bites – but I assure you that a delicate float fishing presentation would show them perfectly.

On large or sparsely populated waters, the fish may spend so little time within float fishing range, that there is small chance of using the float effectively. And when bites are likely to be this infrequent, it will take a very dedicated angler to watch a float for such long periods of time. However, if any angler can learn to be adaptable and to make the most of any opportunities which come his way, he may well be rewarded – and a float may be of real benefit here. Some opportunities come quite unexpectedly, but others, with a little forethought, can be encouraged. Matchmen will bait two or more different areas in a swim, so that if one area stops producing, they always have an alternative; for this very reason, I seldom neglect to bait the margins, just in case, and there is no method better suited to margin fishing than using a float.

Stalking tench can be another productive way of putting a few fish on the bank and, once again, the float can offer enormous benefits. I will never forget one gruelling session I once spent on a notoriously difficult gravel pit; all my best laid plans had come to nothing and my spirit was waning. After another non-productive morning, I decided to take a walk and see if the carp which had been present in a different area were still there. A short stroll would at least offer a break from the monotony of watching my static bobbins slowly fossilise.

The carp had gone, but as I stood there a group of seven big tench moved in close to a marginal bed of ornate miniature lilies. The water was so clear that even at about 8ft, I could see every detail right down to their little red eyes; what's more, they looked as if they were in a feeding mood. Luckily, I had an open tin of sweetcorn and a catapult with me, so I carefully flicked a dozen grains to land beside them: they immediately swam over and began to mop it up greedily.

Quickly but quietly I introduced a few more pouches of bait, then dashed off to collect a rod. In a few very hasty minutes I'd bitten the leger rig off one of my 12ft Avons and replaced it with a little 6in waggler locked onto 5lb line, and a size 12 hook.

The tench were still there, and still had their heads down on the bait. I estimated the depth and set the float so that the bait would lie on the bottom and, after baiting the hook with one large grain, cast it well beyond the fish, then drew it back so that the bait dropped down between them. The float wasn't perfectly cocked, but as far as I could see the bait had settled nicely on the bottom.

Less than two minutes later my rod was hooped into an alarming arc, well beyond its 1lb test curve, and after a furious, spirited battle I slid the net under a personal best float-caught tench. It weighed 8lb 5oz, which was more than enough to lift me out of the doldrums.

The float rig I used was nothing fancy, just a simple, old-fashioned, laying-on sort of style, which is, of course, the basic rig from which almost all stillwater float rigs can be adapted for tench fishing.

Tackle shops sell a vast array of different floats, but there are only a few patterns that I would be likely to use for tench. First there is the Bodied Waggler (Diagram 7, Fig 1), which is ideal except when there is a fair chop on the water. Then I would choose a Driftbeater (Fig 2), which is more stable in windy conditions and incorporates a largish sight bob on the top, making it much easier to see on choppy water. Having a very fine stem also makes it most effective in responding to delicate lift bites.

(top) *Simon Lush and Jim Bigden share the rewards of a magic morning and pose with fish weighing 9lb 5oz, 9lb 2oz, 9lb 1oz, 8lb 13oz and a 7lb 2oz male*
(below) *Jim Bigden with a 9lb 11oz fish, his biggest of five 'nines' to date*

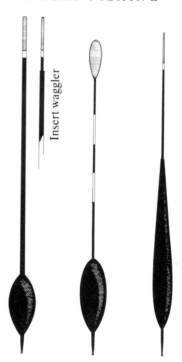

Diagram 7 Floats:
(left) *Waggler*
(centre) *Drift beater*
(right) *Canal Blue*

Insert waggler

The third choice is a delicate canal-type float incorporating a very fine stem which Drennan markets as the Stillwater Blue (Fig 3). These floats are really superb for still conditions when fishing close in, and for ultra-sensitive detection of even the gentlest bites.

Recently I have been converted to Drennan's range of interconnecting Crystal Insert Wagglers. Constructed from clear tubular plastic, they are almost invisible in the water, which must make them less likely to scare fish, especially when stalking in shallow water. Also, they are constructed of interconnecting parts, so all manner of useful variations can be achieved. For instance, put a long insert vane with a wind-beater type sight bob on top of a long straight waggler float body, and a very long but sensitive float can be made, able to stabilise itself below a strong surface tow.

The only other float I am likely to use for tench is a short length of peacock quill, which is perfect for use with the lift method.

There are many different float fishing methods and shotting patterns which are useful for tench, but I tend to rely on just a few well proven methods. Probably the most versatile is the simple laying-on rig (Diagram 8), so we will discuss how this works before considering other float fishing rigs and the various circumstances in which they might be used. Furthermore I am aware that quite a few specialist anglers

Short and chunky, this is my best tench to date, weighing 9lb 8oz

in fact have next to no knowledge of how to go about using a float, so it would be a mistake to become too technical in the assumption that everyone has mastered the basics.

When laying on the float is attached to the line bottom end only and then locked in place by the bulk shot. This allows it to be cast accurately, like a dart, and also enables us to sink the line between the rod-tip and float, thus preventing the effects of wind and surface drift from dragging the float out of place. Back shotting with a

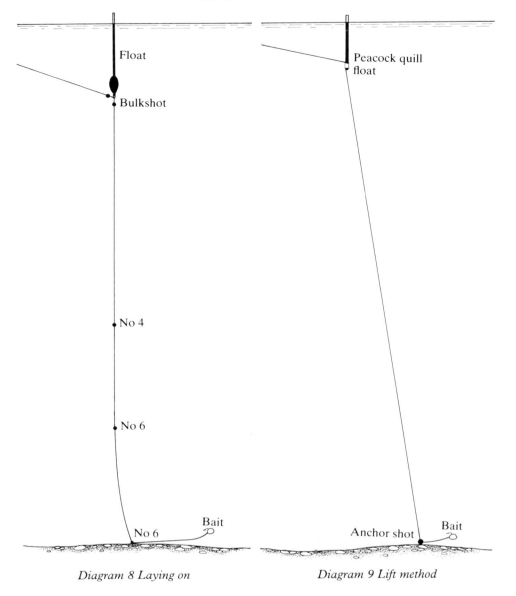

Diagram 8 Laying on   Diagram 9 Lift method

small dust shot a few feet up the line from the float can also help overcome this problem, as will submerging the rod-tip below the surface.

Back to the rig itself: a tell-tale shot is pinched onto the line above the hook, to anchor the bait to the lake bed where it can work by accentuating bite indication. A properly shotted float should be able to register a bite in two ways: first, when a fish swims off with a bait, it should register by pulling a delicate float under. And second, in response to a fish gently lifting a bait, the float should lift in the water; if the tell-tale shot is close to the hook, when the fish picks up the bait, it cannot help but lift the shot as well.

The heavier the tell-tale is, the more pronounced this lift-bite indication will be. Even so, I like to keep the tell-tale shot as light as possible, just heavy enough to anchor the bait to the bottom effectively yet still able to afford a positive lift indication, at the same time avoiding a tell-tale so heavy that it alarms a tench picking up the bait. Depending on conditions and the size of the bait, this shot can be anything from one number 6 shot in very calm conditions, up to one BB or more when there is a fair ripple on the water or larger baits are being used.

Between the bulk shot and the tell-tale, a number of intermediary shot are placed which perform a number of different functions, their size and position depending on how we want a rig to work. Their main function is to help prevent the float from being pulled out of position by surface drift or undertow. The stronger the drift, the larger these shot will need to be in order to counteract it, and the further down the line they will need to be placed.

Unlike match anglers who usually require their float rigs to present a bait so as to pick up fish on the drop, we will seldom need to use any really tiny split shot, as tench seldom intercept a bait in mid-water; I rarely use any smaller than number 4 or 6. However, there will be times when a bait moving slowly across the lake bed will prove more acceptable to tench than a static one. This can be easy enough to achieve when wind or drift conditions are favourable by the simple trick of balancing the weight of the shot against the amount of available drift. Sometimes this will require keeping the shot down the line to a minimum, which is best achieved by using a number 8 shot as a tell-tale.

If you experience regular tangles during casting, one solution is to keep the first intermediary shot down the line a little under half-way up from the hook. Also during casting, trap the line against the lip of the spool with your fore-finger, just before the rig lands in the water; this will force the rig to straighten out and land in a line with the bait beyond the float. Finally, what is the correct distance to set the tell-tale shot above the baited hook? If angling had simple answers, it would be a far more straightforward game – it would also be far less absorbing. There are, of course, so many anomalies that all we can do is start with generalisations and then experiment until we get it right.

As a rule, confidently feeding tench should be an easy proposition when fishing largish baits on the float. Normally bites will be slow and leisurely, so that all we require of a float rig is that it should allow a bite to develop before we strike the hook home. With biggish baits such as breadflake or lobworms, I would opt for a hooklength of between 8in to 1ft between the hook and tell-tale. If confident bites are missed, or if the hookhold is only just in the lips, lengthen the hooklength a little to allow the fish time to pick up the bait properly. On the other hand, if the fish are deeply hooked, then it will need shortening.

When bites are finicky, as they tend to be especially with mass baits such as casters and maggots, many will be missed as the hookbait is picked up and quickly rejected. In these circumstances the hooklength will need to be much shorter in order to facilitate positive indications: three to five inches would be reasonable, though it may be necessary to go shorter still.

One time-honoured way of overcoming tiny bites is the lift method, developed in the fifties by Dick Walker and Fred J. Taylor (Diagram 9). Instead of having the bulk of the weight set up near the float, it is set down at the other end of the rig, next to the hook, where it can work as a heavy tell-tale.

A short length of peacock quill, lacking the buoyancy to support the shot, is fixed onto the line bottom end only with a float band. The float is usually set a little overdepth and anchored with a single SSG swanshot placed a mere inch or so from the hook. After casting, the rod is put in two rodrests and the line tightened until only the tip of the float stands proud of the surface.

Now, when a fish picks up the bait, it cannot avoid also lifting the swanshot from the lake bed. In response, the float should rise instantly and fall flat on the surface. And in practice, while this rig usually produces dramatic bites, your response in striking may have to be lightning quick, as the weight of a swanshot can cause a very speedy rejection of the bait, especially where educated tench are concerned.

In theory, the buoyancy of the float should support most of the weight of the shot when a fish picks up the bait, but in my experience of alarmed fish, this is not completely reliable. Because of this I generally prefer to use a delicately shotted waggler, though weather conditions may prevent such presentations.

When night fishing, the small bite indications you would expect from a delicate rig will be difficult to see. This is when the lift method, by accentuating bites, will offer a real advantage. Providing the float is not too thick, it is easy to attach a beta-light onto it – simply push a short length of supple rig tube onto the top of it, then cut the tube so that 3/8in is left standing proud of the quill, and push your beta-light in firmly.

It is worth investing in the brightest beta-light you can get; anything less than 500 micro-lamberts tends to be difficult to see more than a few rod-lengths out. During the last few seasons I have taken to using a Drennan Night Light, as beta-lights tend to cause optical illusions which can get you striking at nothing at all. Night Lights are much brighter and, even at quite long distances, are easier on the eyes and therefore less likely to cause hallucinations. In fact they are so bright that you can still see them after they have gone under, which can be a problem in itself. Night Lights are designed to fit onto the top of any of the Drennan Insert Crystal Floats as well as his Zoomers, so you don't have to make your own floats.

About fifteen years ago, I did a lot of tench fishing in a very weedy Devonshire canal. The prospects of catching any fish much above 5lb were extremely low, but nevertheless it was an absorbing, productive water and I found the fishing very enjoyable. More importantly, when it came to float fishing in weed, the lessons it taught me were invaluable.

At the beginning of each season, local anglers (and myself) would drag swims out of the dense beds of milfoil and Canadian pondweed. For a while we could catch easily on standard laying-on rigs, but no matter how often the swims were dragged, the weed would soon grow again at an alarming rate and before long get so bad that

Flashback to the mid-seventies: Brian Cannal banks a float-caught fish

the hookbait would invariably catch up before it got down to the bottom. Longer hooklengths were impossible to use, because even if the tell-tale shot did get down, you could never be sure that the hook was not hung up in the weed-stems.

The rig I eventually developed to overcome this (Diagram 10) required a very fine-vaned float such as a Stillwater Blue, which would stand inches clear of the surface if the tell-tale failed to get down to the bottom. By using a number 4 shot as a tell-tale and setting the depth so it was suspended just a fraction off the bottom, I could be confident that, providing the hooklink was kept short (no more than 4in), if the fine stem cocked perfectly the bait had got to the bottom. Obviously this rig only suits the calmest of conditions, and it tends to pick up line-bites; nonetheless it far out-fishes other rigs in these circumstances.

In some waters the weed will eventually grow right up to the surface; when this happens, the tench may refuse to feed in pre-dragged areas, especially in bright conditions, though they may well still be feeding and bubbling away carelessly amidst the weedroots right in the thick of the weedbeds.

Fishing in dense weedbeds should be avoided unless you are reasonably confident of being able to get tench out without damaging their mouths. Anglers must surely take a responsible attitude towards their fish, and avoid taking risks that could result in leaving fish tethered to weed by a broken line; this could result in a horribly slow death, or their mouths being ripped in their efforts to break free.

I am therefore extremely hesitant to reveal the following rig, and I urge that it should only *ever* be used for margin fishing – and even then, only if you are prepared to go in for a fish if it should become tethered.

This approach requires bullying tactics with a long soft-action rod of at least 1¾lb test, and lines of not less than 9lb breaking strain. Such strong lines will not necessarily deter these fish from accepting the bait, as they are unlikely to be feeding cautiously in what they must consider a safe haven. A large, strong hook of not less than size 10 is also recommended, as anything smaller may tear the mouth.

The technique is to bomb a bait straight down through the weed stems to the bubblers amongst the roots, and the rig I use to do this (Diagram 11) is virtually the same as the standard lift method. The only real difference is that the float supports the weight of the shot, which will need to be at least one SSG in order to get the bait down quickly. I set the float to support the shot just an inch or so off the bottom. It may take several attempts to get the bait down without it getting caught up, but once through, the float should cock precisely. Bites must be hit instantly, and the fish played mercilessly up to the surface and quickly hassled into the net before it can bolt off deep into the weed.

It is dubious if this approach can be called sporting – moreover it can easily backfire, forcing you to go in after your fish. All the same, it can be very effective when all else fails.

On the whole, big fish specialists have failed to develop float fishing to anywhere near the level of sophistication achieved in legering. However, there is no reason

FLOAT FISHING

why a float cannot be very successfully used in conjunction with braided or multi-strand hooklinks, hair-rigs or pop-up baits, thereby incorporating the superior bait presentation possibilities of these with the infinitely superior bite indication provided by a float. All it needs is the willingness to break away from the habitual trap of Optonic mania, coupled with a small pinch of imagination.

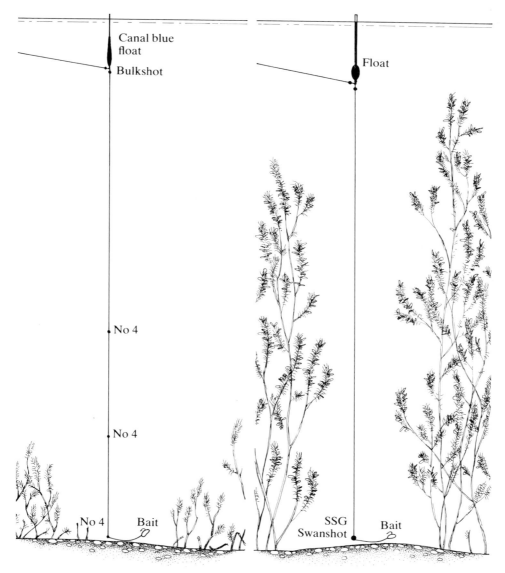

Canal blue float

Bulkshot

Float

No 4

No 4

No 4   Bait

SSG Swanshot   Bait

Diagram 10 Canal blue rig   *Diagram 11 Bombing through weed rig*

4

LEGERING

While float fishing provides an aesthetically pleasing method and offers the ultimate in bite indication, it is in fact undeniable that most of the time on most big tench waters, legering will prove far more useful and versatile.

While a float may cope perfectly with short-range fishing situations, many productive features may be beyond the distance to which it can be cast. Another consideration in favour of legering is that while there may occasionally be hectic moments when the fish have really got their heads down on the baits, there are likely to be long periods of inactivity which can often last a few days and which inevitably defy the sustained concentration required to watch a float. Effective legering methods can take the strain out of these situations, and will usually prove more practical and versatile. Which is exactly why it has taken such a prominent place in stillwater specimen hunting over the years!

Forty years ago legering was considered a crude method, but over the years it has developed into a highly complex art. However, many anglers seem to confuse the fundamental principles involved in these advances; they are not sure what they are trying to achieve with their rigs, and do not effectively implement them. I feel it may be pertinent, therefore, to include a brief consideration of these fundamental principles.

All tench legering techniques rely on two underlying principles. The first is to create a very sensitive, resistance-free presentation which allows bites to register as a natural progression on the bite indicator. The second works in exactly the opposite way: after a fish has picked up the bait, the rig should create sufficient resistance that the fish is panicked into bolting and, by so doing, hooks itself against the weight of the lead.

RUNNING LEGERS

When I was a lad, all my legering was with a simple running leger (Diagram 12) using swingtips or silver foil bobbins for bite indication. The lake I fished had a very soft silty bottom, into which the lead must have sunk rather deeply, even though we never used any heavier than 1/2 oz. Bites were nearly always fast and positive, quite different to the leisurely affairs experienced while float fishing, and even then I questioned why the two methods should provoke such different responses. With hindsight, however, it is obvious that because the lead had sunk into the silt, it created sufficient resistance to alarm a fish after it had picked up the bait. This would panic it into either rejecting the bait or otherwise bolting off with it. Hence the speed of the bites.

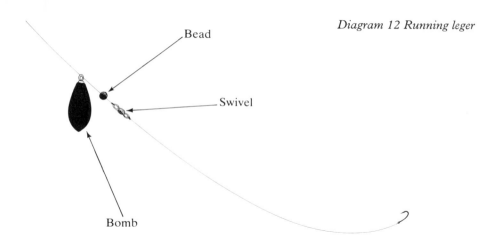

Diagram 12 Running leger

Bead

Swivel

Bomb

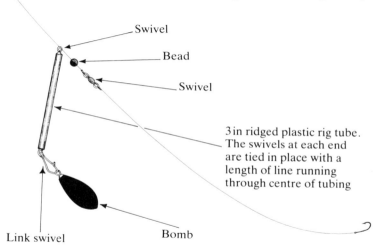

Diagram 13 Running link leger

Swivel

Bead

Swivel

3 in ridged plastic rig tube.
The swivels at each end
are tied in place with a
length of line running
through centre of tubing

Link swivel

Bomb

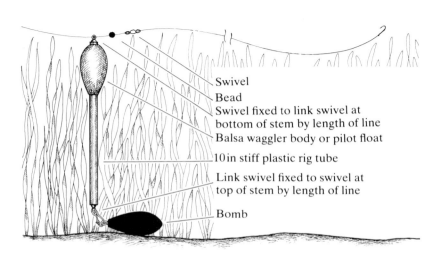

Swivel
Bead
Swivel fixed to link swivel at
bottom of stem by length of line
Balsa waggler body or pilot float

10 in stiff plastic rig tube

Link swivel fixed to swivel at
top of stem by length of line

Bomb

*Diagram 14
Buoyant stick leger*

I can only speculate how many times baits were rejected, but I do remember eventually increasing my catch rate on still days, not by watching the indicator but rather the point at which the line entered the water. The tiniest pulls, barely discernible on even a swingtip, were slightly exaggerated on the surface of the water and when struck at, often accounted for a fish which otherwise might not have ended up on the bank.

Since those early days I have experimented with all kinds of variations on a running leger theme, including incorporating a short-running legerlink (Diagram 13). Now, while I believe a link can improve this system, my conclusions are that in terms of achieving maximum sensitivity, all running legers leave a lot to be desired.

In theory, they should work well enough on a clean lake bed, especially when a fish pulls directly away from you. In practice however, the lake bed is seldom clear of weed, filamentous algae or patches of silt; furthermore at longer range, the line between the lead and the rod may be lying across gravel bars or weedbeds, all of which will inhibit the free movement of line through the lead.

Because of these shortcomings I rarely use running legers or link legers, except when fishing close in – and even then, only where the bottom is clean. Occasionally I resort to using a long buoyant stick legerlink; the purpose of this rig (Diagram 14) is to try to keep the free-running swivel up off the bottom in areas where it is carpeted by weed or filamentous algae. Care must be taken to tighten up very gently after casting, otherwise the buoyant link will be pulled down into the weed, which will block free passage of the line through the swivel and render the whole technique useless.

PATERNOSTERS

Back in the mid-seventies, the objective of creating minimum resistance and maximum sensitivity became all-important amongst specimen anglers. Many turned to the paternoster, the favoured system of match anglers on waters such as the Fens. This system (Diagram 15) maximised sensitivity by making the pull direct to the rod so a fish didn't have to pull the line through the lead itself.

For my money, there isn't a more sensitive system than a fixed paternoster. Many anglers incorporate the use of a running paternoster link (Diagram 16) but it is debatable how many real advantages this system offers. It allows a fish accepting the bait to move off without towing the lead, but it can occasionally tangle and therefore cannot be relied on to run freely – and even if it could, I can see no positive advantage over a fixed paternoster where tench are concerned.

One of the most interesting things about angling is how many of us seem to disagree over some of the most basic objectives, and this is especially true when it comes to rig design and bait presentation. And judging by the conflicting articles written on legering for tench, this is one area which is rife with opposing opinions, and nowhere more so than in the mechanics of a simple fixed paternoster.

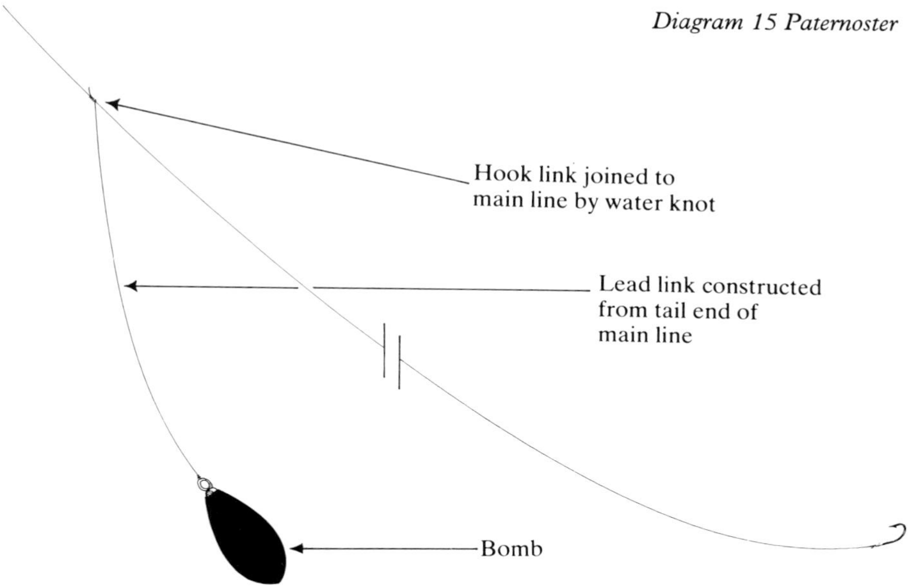

Diagram 15 Paternoster

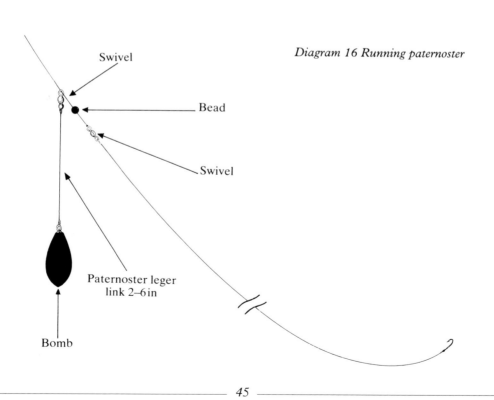

Hook link joined to
main line by water knot

Lead link constructed
from tail end of
main line

Bomb

Diagram 16 Running paternoster

Swivel

Bead

Swivel

Paternoster leger
link 2–6in

Bomb

Most of us agree that confident takes can be tackled by using a relatively short distance between the hook and the lead, while finicky bites can be encouraged into bigger pulls, simply by increasing that distance. However, it seems we all disagree about the best way to do that. Eric Edwards in the NASA magazine *Specialist Angler* No. 5 describes the use of a 2ft legerlink, tied to a 2in hooklink. Len Arbery in his book *Catching Big Tench* starts off with a 3ft legerlink, tied to an 18in hooklink. Len Head in *Tench* advises an 18in legerlink, tied to a hooklink of at least 3ft and up to 5ft or more. A confusing difference of opinion!

The objective of all these rigs is to turn twitches into decent pulls but I believe we must first identify why the fish are twitching in the first place. By and large they do so for two totally different reasons. One is when we are using a quantity of particle baits and they are feeding confidently, but don't need to move off with the bait (obviously you would not expect them to give big bites). The other reason is when they have become rig- and/or bait-shy. Although they want the bait, they are rejecting the hookbaits; this is usually done by feeling for resistance. My own view is that these two different situations require fundamentally different rig designs to deal with them effectively.

Let us first consider the second of these situations. Is it possible to devise a rig offering sensitivity which also overcomes problems of resistance? Assuming the swim is not full of weed, a long legerlink will certainly minimise resistance

A 7lb 2½oz estate-lake fish which I took on long-range feeder tactics

However, unless the fish pulls directly away from the rod, it will not provide any great measure of sensitivity.

To prove this, try the following simple experiment: first set up a rod with a swingtip and tie a leger on to the end of the line. Next, tie two loops in the line, one 4in up from the lead and the other 3ft from the lead; these will represent two alternative legerlinks. Straighten the line until the swingtip hangs in a normal fishing position, then go to the lead and experiment by pulling the loops in various directions. By pulling them away from the rod, you will notice that there is no difference between them – either way a 6in pull will lift the swingtip 6in. However, when you pull them at right angles, it becomes evident that with the short legerlink a 2in pull pivots off the lead, is efficiently transferred to the swingtip and moves it considerably. With the long legerlink, a 2in pull barely makes the tip tremble – while offering little resistance, it also offers little sensitivity and is unlikely to register twitches effectively. The short link on the other hand gives greater sensitivity, but the resistance caused by the lead will be encountered quite quickly.

The length of the legerlink therefore offers us a choice: long links for overcoming resistance, or short links for sensitivity. While the restriction caused by the lead may seem a disadvantage, in my experience it not only makes for better bite registration, but can also, once the line has been pulled up hard against it, provide a bolt rig facility which increases the potential of the rig.

Some tench anglers rely on the use of ultra-sensitive indication systems, such as swingtips, to overcome twitches. Now, while twitches can certainly be dealt with this way, I would argue that very often it us using long legerlinks which *creates* the problems which require such sensitive indicators.

With a short legerlink, when a fish moves off with a bait, the link will primarily offer a more sensitive indication, despite the fact that it will quickly pull up against the resistance of the lead. A long legerlink seeks to prevent this happening, but fails to offer any real advantages in doing so.

In order to get maximum efficiency out of a rig, the relationship between the hook and the lead must be manipulated so it works for *you*. For a start, I am convinced that a long hooklink induces confidence in nervous fish. A long legerlink will only introduce a slow build-up of resistance and so will not help to achieve this aim; but with a long hooklink, a fish can move a considerable distance before feeling any resistance – it therefore builds up confidence as it takes up the slack hooklink available. Consequently, as soon as its pull begins to pivot off the short legerlink, we are more likely to get a reasonably confident indication.

Match anglers use this approach all the time, especially when bream fishing. The principle behind it being if you give fish enough line, they will hang themselves.

Conservation is becoming an increasingly important issue in angling. Carp anglers know just how much their favourite species is worth, in terms of money and of growth years. A single fish dying from angling mishaps, especially a big one, can seriously reduce the potential of a fishery, and this is as true with tench as it is with carp.

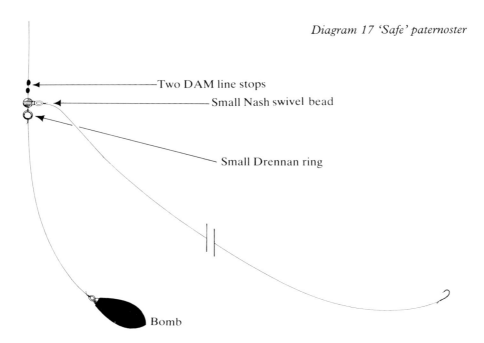

Diagram 17 'Safe' paternoster

Two DAM line stops

Small Nash swivel bead

Small Drennan ring

Bomb

As a result, carp anglers have modified their rigs to reduce any dangers inherent in their use, especially with fixed lead systems, and tench specialists are slowly following suit. Few rigs are potentially more devastating than a fixed paternoster: should it snap off above the knot which joins the two links, it will leave the fish towing the rig about until inevitably it becomes tethered to weedbeds or submerged snags. I eventually adapted a carp-rig idea in order to prevent this potential problem (Diagram 17), but without losing the benefits of a fixed paternoster link.

BOLT RIGS AND SELF-HOOKING DEVELOPMENTS

During the last decade or so, many developments have filtered out of the carp scene to be adapted successfully by tench anglers; they have now become an integral part of modern tench fishing.

The success of these rigs is dependent on a fish moving off with the bait, then pulling up against the weight of a fixed lead, thereby hooking itself. A very sharp hook is vital, used in conjunction with a hefty lead of at least 1½ oz. Once pricked, a tench will either bolt, or stay put and try to reject the hook. However, provided a reasonably sensitive indication system is used, the fish should move it enough to galvanise you into whacking it.

It is said that because tench have a very delicate style of feeding and are highly intolerant of resistance, self-hooking systems are ineffective, and that tench caught on them are caught in spite of and not because of the rigs. Undoubtedly I am not the first angler to think that it is precisely because of their delicate style of feeding that these rigs can be used effectively; surely any pull which is big enough to twitch an indicator, no matter how sensitive, should be big enough to pull the hooklink straight to a fixed lead and cause the tench to prick itself.

Time after time my friends and I have used this approach *because* it can convert twitchers into churners – and our catches do stand up to scrutiny! These rigs will not necessarily convert every pick-up into a fish on the bank, but then neither will hovering over the rods and swatting every flicker of the indicators. Twitcher-hitting may be acceptable during short sessions, but when the interval between bites is many hours or even days, it is not practical to stare expectantly at indicators which refuse to move. Anyway, it is Sod's Law that you stare at them until your attention wavers, turn to pick up the flask and miss a bite. During long sessions it is impossible to focus the attention throughout, and this is where efficient self-hooking rigs become invaluable. Certainly on 'pressured' waters tench eventually become wary of rigs and try to avoid getting hooked, but a little experimentation has always overcome the problem.

We can also employ these rigs when fishing mass baits. I proposed earlier that twitching is very often caused when tench are feeding on a profusion of tiny food items; this method of baiting encourages them to graze on pockets of bait in a small area before moving on, rather than darting deliberately from bait to bait. The more bait you put in, however, the more problematic it becomes, because although you can attract a lot of fish into the swim by mass baiting, spotting the bites can be a nightmare. Educated tench especially will reject baited hooks long before they are alarmed by resistance, simply because the hookbaits behave differently from the other items. When this happens, probably all you will know about it is that the hookbaits come back squashed or mis-shapen – maggots may be stretched rather than pulped, and casters broken or flattened.

Obviously long hooklinks only accentuate this problem. Generally short hooklinks would ensure that bites are indicated, but would tend to register as twitches. However, introducing a self-hooking principle would turn most of them into flyers. A carp angler's bolt rig (Diagram 18) combining a very short hooklink would usually have little application in tench fishing, but in this situation it could prove unbeatable.

Before discussing these developments further, we should consider the morality of self-hooking rigs, an area which has after all, drawn scorn from some factions of the angling fraternity. A proportion of this negativity is born of ignorance. However, these views are constantly reinforced by the antics of a number of thoughtless louts who insist on leaving their rods to fish for themselves, while they wander the banks, bars and even nightclubs.

These rigs can be deadly in more than one way. While nothing is to be gained by reverting to any of the ineffective rigs we laboured with in the past, it is vital that we

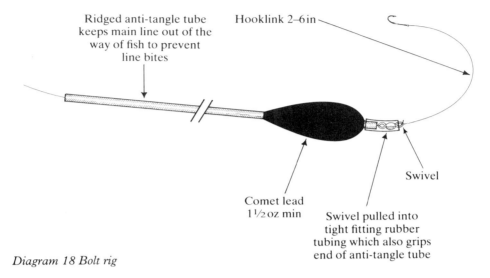

Ridged anti-tangle tube keeps main line out of the way of fish to prevent line bites

Hooklink 2–6 in

Comet lead 1½ oz min

Swivel

Swivel pulled into tight fitting rubber tubing which also grips end of anti-tangle tube

Diagram 18 Bolt rig

do not abuse the new advances by leaving the rods unattended. One thing you can rely on is that a self-hooked tench will power deeply into weedroots or snags. Once there, it will be very difficult to get out and will be at risk of becoming tethered, with dire consequences.

My own application of these rigs started in the early eighties, when the carp lads were picking up a disproportionate number of big tench on boilies. Soon enough line clips, hair rigs, braided hooklinks, backstops, fixed leads and anti-tangle rigs filtered into my tench fishing. At first, most of these developments were merely imitations of the carp anglers' rigs – there was little need to improve them as the tench were naive and consequently got caught; but as they slowly wised up, we had to experiment so as to keep one step ahead. Basically this meant applying tench rig principles to the new rigs.

The principle of long hooklinks, once again, proved more effective with boilies than the short hooklinks used by the carp lads. Once that had been sorted out, my friends and I caught far more tench than the carp anglers did. Softer baits accounted partly for this, but long hooklinks completed the story. Funnily enough, we were also probably catching as many carp as they were, though our tongue-in-cheek references to these as 'nuisance fish' did little for our social standing!

Ultimately our successful rigs consisted of 18in braided links, with the leads back-stopped by a powergun stop-knot a few inches up the line (Diagram 19). A 1½ in looped hair constructed from 1lb b.s. mono tied to the bend of the hook, completed the rig.

This most unlikely set-up – popularly known as the 'hang-up hair rig' – worked admirably for a remarkable length of time. However, the tench did eventually learn to pick up the bait but avoid the hook. Unbelievably we then began to experience full-blooded runs which resulted in striking into thin air. We moved on to fixed leads and tying the hair anti-eject style off the eye of the hook, constructing it from the tab end of the braided hook-knot. For a season or two this usually overcame the problem, although often the hooklink needed lengthening a little.

Once again it was only a matter of time before bites failed to materialise into fish on the bank. By then we were experiencing a number of knocks on the rod-tip as the fish learned to feel for resistance. At first these knocks were mistaken for line bites, but the truth became obvious when they occasionally resulted in a hooked fish if struck. At this time even some of the full-blooded churners resulted in fish dropping off when landed.

To overcome this we learned to present the bait backed up close to the eye of the hook, which made it almost impossible for the tench to pick it up and avoid the hook. Also it helped to make ejection rather difficult. And in an attempt to overcome their caution, the hooklink was further increased to over 3ft and occasionally up to as much as 5ft. Simon Lush was the first of my fishing partners to use this rig (Diagram 20): little did he know what the outcome would be.

It had been a long week and Simon had suffered a number of problems with twitches. Tench were obviously present in the area, and after much frustration he managed to winkle out a beauty of 8lb 11oz. Eventually he got the rig sorted out, but little did he know how well it would work. The next morning he landed his first-ever 'nine', which should have been reward enough; but by lunchtime he had surpassed all his dreams with fish weighing 9lb 3oz, 9lb 1oz, 8lb 13oz, and a male of 7lb 2oz.

Since then this rig has more or less become our standard method and has worked in every water we have used it. On unpressured waters I tend to keep the hooklink short, about 18in, only lengthening it for more 'wary' fish. There is evidence however, that on one or two waters the fish are learning to move away for no more than a few inches with a bait. Obviously the only solution is to go to the opposite extreme and use very short hooklinks of no longer than 2 or 3in. During recent seasons my fishing has focussed on unexploited waters where sophisticated approaches are unnecessary; I have therefore asked Len Arbery to expand on this theme in his chapter 'The Long Life Pit'.

One last recommendation: that once cast out, longer hooklinks should be left where they land and not pulled back to straighten out the rig. The rig should fall in a heap on the lake bed, with the bait dropping close to the lead. This will help instil confidence in a fish by allowing it to move a fair way in any direction before it comes up against the resistance of the lead.

HAIR RIGS AND RECENT HOOK PRESENTATION DEVELOPMENTS

The hair rig has proved invaluable in tench fishing, once its initial problems were sorted out, and is especially useful in overcoming twitches. Its main benefit is that because the hook is outside the bait it is not easily ejected, once picked up, without the hook lodging in the mouth. Diagram 21 shows a variety of methods used to mount the bait on a hair; the top row shows the presentations I have used successfully, in chronological order.

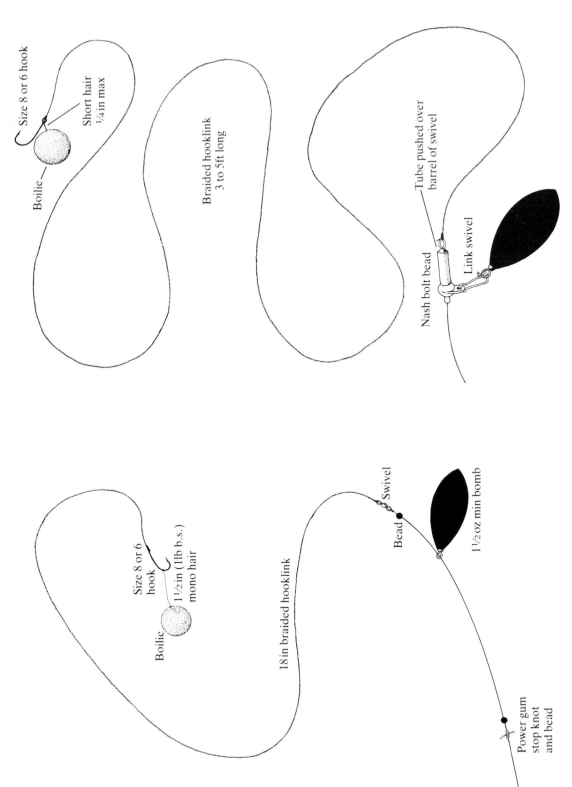

Size 8 or 6 hook

Short hair
1/4 in max

Boilie

Braided hooklink
3 to 5ft long

Tube pushed over
barrel of swivel

Nash bolt bead

Link swivel

Diagram 20 Long hooklink with fixed lead

Size 8 or 6
hook

1 1/2 in (1lb b.s.)
mono hair

Boilie

18in braided hooklink

Swivel

Bead

1 1/2 oz min bomb

Power gum
stop knot
and bead

Diagram 19 Hang-up hair rig

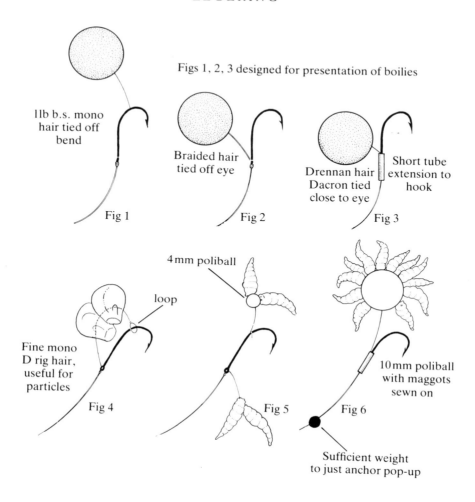

1lb b.s. mono
hair tied off
bend

Figs 1, 2, 3 designed for presentation of boilies

Braided hair
tied off eye

Drennan hair
Dacron tied
close to eye

Short tube
extension to
hook

Fig 1

Fig 2

Fig 3

4mm poliball

loop

Fine mono
D rig hair,
useful for
particles

10mm poliball
with maggots
sewn on

Fig 4

Fig 5

Fig 6

Sufficient weight
to just anchor pop-up

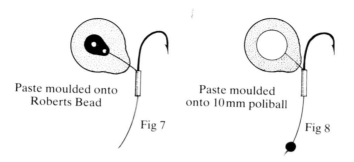

Paste moulded onto
Roberts Bead

Paste moulded
onto 10mm poliball

Fig 7

Fig 8

Diagram 21 Hair rig adaptations

My own conclusions are that the distance between the bait and the hook is best kept short and compact. Compared to big carp, tench have small mouths and do not seem to suck boilies up to crush them in the pharyngeals as carp do; they tend to pick them up and hold them just inside the mouth. Therefore nothing can be gained by tying a long hair; between 1/4 and 1/2 in from hook to bait should be more than ample, making it difficult for a tench to pick up the bait without taking the hook inside its lips.

Fig 3 shows the hair rig pattern I like best. A short length of clear supple rig tube is slipped over the eye of the hook, setting the hair slightly down the shank and therefore slightly extending the hook. This ensures that when the bait is sucked in, the hook follows it into the fish's mouth bend first. Once in, because of the close positioning of the hair to the eye, it becomes difficult for the fish to eject the bait without the hook following it in the correct position to prick the lip.

I prefer to use the smallest practical hook to avoid weighing the bait down. Size 8s will usually be perfect for use with 16mm boilies, size 10 for 10mm baits and size 12 for 6mm baits.

Also included in Diagram 21 are a number of useful hair rig systems which I have used effectively with baits other than boilies.

POP-UPS AND NEUTRAL BUOYANCY BAITS

Buoyant boilies, or pop-ups, have proved highly effective for tench. Indeed, in some of the weedier swims, they are the only practical way of presenting a bait. Obviously it is always preferable to present baits in clear areas, as a hair rig can hardly be expected to work properly if it is caught up in weed. Unfortunately circumstances do not always present the luxury of clear areas, and if the fish are present in weed and aren't prepared to come out, the only option is to go in after them. One way of doing this with a boilie is to make it float and then pop it up over the top of the weed (Diagram 22). This rig may look like a very odd method of presentation, but looks can be deceiving and in practice the rig has often worked where all else failed.

There are several ways of making buoyant boilies. They can be grilled or micro-waved so they expand and dry out, or they can be doctored by using a Marvic Boilie Punch to inject a foam insert. The most effective method is to make baits with a small polyball inserted into a number of them; this method also helps to preserve the flavour.

Pop-ups are not limited to weedbed presentations, of course. In open water I pre-fer to balance baits precisely so that they only just sink, and so that the anchor-weight on the hooklink rests on the bottom. Now the bait will hover gently above it at a predetermined distance – usually 1 to 3in will be ample.

It all came right in the end! Simon Lush with two 9s, an 8 and a 7lb male

A popular theory in support of pop-up baits in carp fishing is that their neutral buoyancy allows them to waft about attractively in the disturbance created by feeding carp. Feeding tench, however, seldom create the volume of disturbance needed to do this. Nevertheless pop-ups do seem to hold a very strong visual attraction to tench, partly because they do not sink into the silt, algae or weed. Also, because a pop-up bait is naturally inclined to float upwards, when a fish sucks at it, it is much more likely to rocket straight into its mouth.

I spent some time experimenting with pop-ups presented on a bent-hook hair rig constructed from size 10 and 8 Drennan Lure Hooks: these trials were successful, but I am yet to be convinced of the superiority of this set-up (Diagram 23, Fig 1). Actually I would prefer to conduct further field tests, before commenting further. One thing that deeply concerns me however, is that this rig has a disturbing tendency to become double embedded in the fish's mouth, causing unacceptable damage. Fig 2 shows a presentation which has worked just as effectively for me. Intrinsically it is identical to my bottom bait set-up; however, in order for it to work most effectively, the bait must be so buoyant that it forces the hook to stand up rather than flop about beneath it.

Neutral buoyancy baits provide a subtle refinement to the pop-up theme by incorporating less buoyant baits with the intention of neutralising the weight of the hook and overcoming cautious feeding. There are numerous ways of achieving this, both with single and double baits (Diagram 24). One of the easiest ways to reduce buoyancy is by incorporating less polystyrene into the bait and then, after mounting it on the hair, gently squeezing excess air out until it just balances the hook.

ANTI-TANGLE PRESENTATIONS

Braided hooklinks have the advantage of being supple in comparison with the springiness of monofilament. Unfortunately this supple quality creates a tendency for it to tangle with the rig in mid-cast.

Anti-tangle tubing provides one solution to these tangles and its effectiveness in carp fishing is well documented. However, because our hooklinks are usually rather long, the anti-tangle tube needs to be ridiculously long to offer any benefit, and their combined length leads to casting difficulties. The best method I know of overcoming tangles is to use the helicopter rig, and I now use it for virtually all braided links (Diagram 25). This rather ingenious system allows the bait to spin the hooklink around the lead in mid-cast to prevent it tangling.

With long 8lb b.s. Silkworm links, even this rig will still not be 100 per cent effective – I doubt that any rig ever could – so it pays to keep an eye on it in mid-cast. However, including a small PVA stringer (Diagram 26) will help eliminate tangles; it will also ensure that a few free bait samples accompany and increase the attractiveness of the hookbaits.

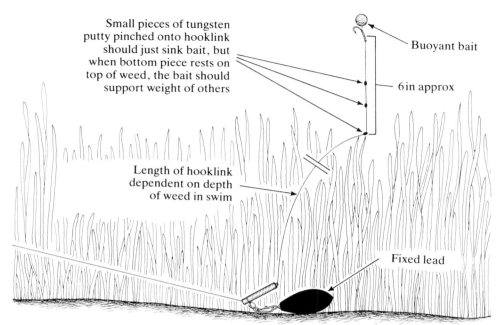

Small pieces of tungsten putty pinched onto hooklink should just sink bait, but when bottom piece rests on top of weed, the bait should support weight of others

Buoyant bait

6 in approx

Length of hooklink dependent on depth of weed in swim

Fixed lead

Diagram 22 Above weed pop-up presentation

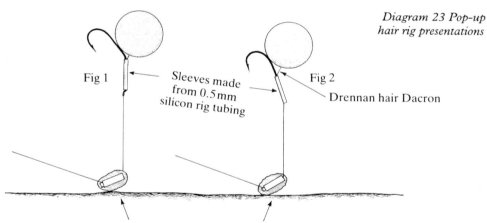

Diagram 23 Pop-up hair rig presentations

Fig 1

Sleeves made from 0.5 mm silicon rig tubing

Fig 2

Drennan hair Dacron

Anchors made from 10mm lengths of 3mm rig tubing plugged with end of cocktail stick, which supports just enough tungsten putty to anchor bait

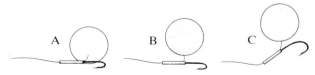

A   B   C

A. Bait only slightly more buoyant than free samples, lies on lake bed but helps to neutralise weight of hook

Diagram 24 Neutral buoyancy presentations

B. Bait hovers above lake bed without lifting hook

C. Bait hovers above lake bed and almost lifts hook

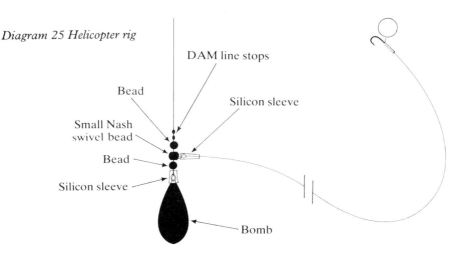

Diagram 25 Helicopter rig

DAM line stops

Bead

Silicon sleeve

Small Nash swivel bead

Bead

Silicon sleeve

Bomb

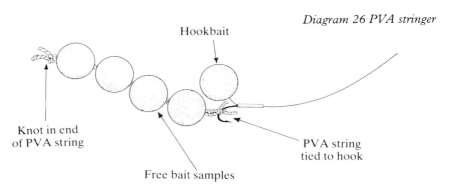

Diagram 26 PVA stringer

Hookbait

Knot in end of PVA string

Free bait samples

PVA string tied to hook

BITE INDICATION SYSTEMS

Commercially available monkey climbers have penetrated most fields of stillwater specimen fishing. Many gravel pits have high banks which prevent anglers from sitting close to the water, and as a result lines stretch out and are buffeted by every gust of wind, causing constant bleeps from the buzzers. Therefore unless it is a flat calm, monkeys would seem to be the only practicable indication system. However, when it comes to spotting bites, monkeys put us at a serious disadvantage. They may well look good, meticulously lined up on stainless steel needles, but in fact they create so much resistance, and are therefore so insensitive, that their validity in tenching is questionable, other than in the aforementioned situations.

For most of my tenching I prefer to use old-fashioned clip-on bobbins (Diagram 27), which are much more sensitive than monkeys. Also, because they clip directly onto the line, they move twice as far in response to a bite than any bobbin designed to let line run through it. Obviously this offers a tremendous advantage when bites lack boldness, because the movements of a clip-on bobbin will be far more positive and therefore easier to interpret.

Surface drift and undertow can prove to be a problem, especially when fishing at long range. To overcome this it may be necessary to pinch swanshot onto the retaining cord under the bobbin. One or two are usually enough to stop the drift from slowly dragging the bobbin up to the rod, though at times I've had to use as many as seven shot. This sounds a lot, but providing they only just balance against the drag they do not cause problems.

When terminal rigs are working effectively, indication systems will be of secondary importance. Nevertheless it can take a period of trial and error before we get the rigs right, so sensitive indicators remain very important in helping to assess what is going on when bites fail to result in fish on the bank. Even if nine bites out of ten set the bobbins flying, there will always be odd knocks which need registering.

Even with self-hooking rigs, a pricked fish can try to eject the hook, rather than bolt. Carp anglers using monkeys have sought to overcome this problem by setting the rod tips high in the rests, so that the tips will register knocks and twitches that the monkeys miss. A clip-on bobbin however, set a few inches below the rod, not only gives a better visual indication of these knocks, but will sound the buzzer, too.

Experience shows there will be occasions when the fish just will not give a decent pull. Nor is it always easy to find out why, or to work out how to overcome it; so, when bites are not developing, it pays to sit on the rods and strike at any indications.

When even clip-on bobbins fail to show adequate bite indications, the only alternative may be to use swingtips (Diagram 28). Swingtips as a method require intense concentration. When bites are coming regularly, they provide a very effective and enjoyable method of fishing – indeed, when conditions suit, they will register bites which other indicators would struggle to show. However, they can prove impossible to use in high winds.

Len Arbery is the keenest advocate of swingtips I know, and who can argue with his results? Therefore rather than cover this subject here, I have left him to describe their use in his chapter 'The Long Life Pit'.

Do not think that I dislike swingtipping; during short morning or evening sessions it can offer a fascinating and enjoyable approach; nevertheless I still regard it as a last resort. My reasoning is that on most of the big tench waters I fish, although one occasionally experiences periods of intense activity, all too often bites come too infrequently to make the use of swingtips sensible. I am therefore more likely to place my confidence in maximising the efficiency of my rigs.

In fact on many pits, high banks make swingtipping virtually impossible – and when there is a strong blow on the water, with the rods bouncing about in the rests and endless clumps of weed drifting into the line, monkey climbers are really the only viable proposition. Then you have no option but to rely on the rigs doing their stuff.

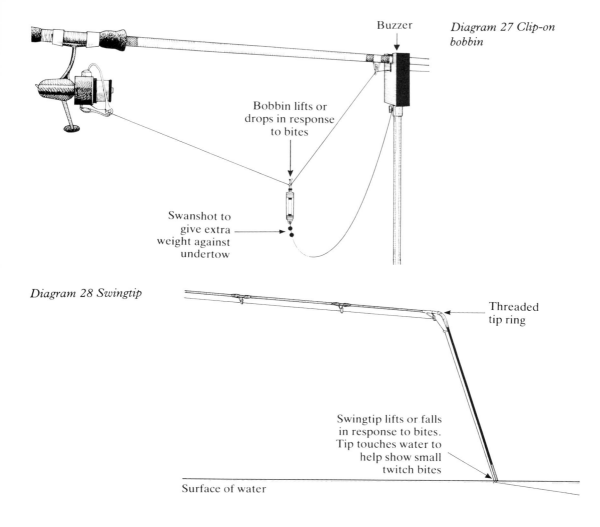

Buzzer

Diagram 27 Clip-on bobbin

Bobbin lifts or drops in response to bites

Swanshot to give extra weight against undertow

Diagram 28 Swingtip

Threaded tip ring

Swingtip lifts or falls in response to bites. Tip touches water to help show small twitch bites

Surface of water

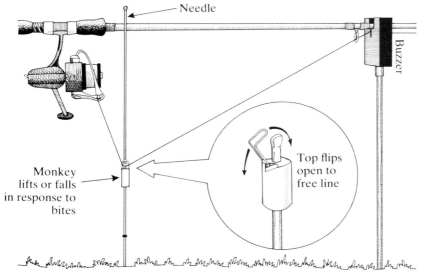

Needle

Buzzer

Monkey lifts or falls in response to bites

Top flips open to free line

Diagram 29 Flip-top PTFE monkey climber

Over the years I have collected and used monkeys of many different shapes and sizes, but eventually have settled for just a few favourites. I require them to be heavy enough to cope with drift and undertow without sliding up the needle, and also heavy enough to drop like a stone in response to drop-back bites. However, at the same time they must still be light enough to be as responsive as possible.

My favourite monkeys are some flip-top PTFE models which I got from Penge Angling in south London (Diagram 29). These super little bobbins are designed in such a way that when the rod is lifted, the wire loop line-retainer flips over to release the line; they thus eliminate any chance of the line catching up during the strike. This problem is a design fault inherent in many PTFE monkeys, which could result in the line breaking. This has never actually happened to me, although on numerous occasions the strike has resulted in non-release of the line – once with a 32lb carp on the end, and once with an 8lb 14oz tench!

SWIMFEEDERS

It seems to me that many tench anglers have stopped using swimfeeders. If this is the case I find it very odd, because ten years ago feeders were the 'in' method. In fact no tackle item ever had a more revolutionary effect on tench fishing, which makes it all the more surprising that so many anglers have forsaken it. Certainly if I had to choose one method with which to do all my tench fishing, I would not hesitate in choosing the feeder: never has there been a more convenient way to deliver both feed and hookbaits on a little and often basis, in the same place, at the same time and with such accuracy.

This demise is probably due to the fact that on many tench waters it is boilies which have become the 'in' method. The fact is though, that some waters have been constantly bombarded with boilies for so long now that the effectiveness of these is beginning to wane considerably. Johnson's, for instance, has seen well over a decade of boilies and their effective use seems to be tailing off. Really, this is inevitable because ultimately, no matter what their flavour or colour, all boilies are just little round balls which eventually spell one thing – trouble! Jim Murrey is one of the long-time regulars on that water, and he informed me that during September 1988 he took numerous sevens using swimfeeders and maggots, while boilies produced only a few reluctant fish to other anglers.

While tench may not be the most intelligent of creatures, given time they will learn to recognise as dangerous a situation they have have confronted often. When the particular method starts showing diminishing returns, intelligent anglers start ringing the changes. Most tend to look for something new, but it is often worth recalling past methods – it may well have been so long since feeders were used, that the fish will have forgotten all about them and will therefore be very vulnerable to them again.

Rigs for effective feeder fishing need not be any different to those used for other legering approaches. My own preference is for fixed paternosters, using exactly the same principles as outlined earlier (p44).

When using maggots as bait, the feederlinks manufactured by Peter Drennan, Thamesly or Middy are perfect. Some anglers complain that during hot summer days, when the maggots are at their liveliest, they tend to escape from the feeder too quickly. Baiting the hook before you fill the feeder can help prevent this; or wrap some black insulating tape around the bottom half of the feeder – this will greatly reduce the speed at which the maggots exit. However, I seldom feel the need to do this, as in my experience, the faster the feeder empties into the swim the more effective it is likely to be.

For most feeder fishing I generally prefer open-ended feeders (Diagram 29), simply because they are more versatile; they can present a variety of mass baits such as maggots and casters, as well as larger particles like sweetcorn and even mini-boilies. They can also be used to lay a carpet of feed quickly by the simple expedient of repeat casting.

The secret of success with open-ended feeders is the consistency of the groundbait used to plug the ends: it should be mixed as dry as possible, only just

Nick Cosford is overjoyed with this 9lb 15oz, his first 7lb-plus tench

damp enough to hold the bait in. I always use brown breadcrumb because its bran content makes it less sticky than white crumb and therefore less likely to clog the feeder. Some shops which specialise in catering for match anglers sell a very coarse brown crumb; when used either on its own or cut with finer crumb this will help disperse the bait very quickly.

If the consistency is right, the groundbait plugs should explode out almost as soon as the feeder splashes down in the water. This will ensure that it empties by the time it hits the bottom and that the contents fall slowly down to settle around the hookbait. While this is easily achieved at up to fifty yards or so, longer casts present more problems because the feeder will require packing more firmly to prevent it losing its contents in mid-air, due to the casting force required to launch it.

Accurate casting is essential for feeder work. I usually start a session by using the feeder to lay down a fair carpet of feed, and I do this before tying the hooklinks on, otherwise they tend to get tangled. Half-a-dozen casts per rod is usually ample. By striking a second or so after the feeder splashes down, a good spread will be ensured; it will also serve as a test that the groundbait is mixed to the right consistency and is not too sticky. Practice makes perfect – if you cannot feel the feeder release its cargo instantly upon striking it out, the consistency is not dry enough, or you are packing it too tightly.

Feeder fishing can be tremendously exciting, and can result in some furious action once the tench home in on the baited area. On occasions it is possible to get the fish actively and hungrily competing with one another, bites sometimes coming so quickly that I have known them intercept the hookbait on the drop. They even learn to associate the feeder's splash with food and quickly home in on it. Not that this situation can be expected to last, as a few repeat captures will teach them caution. When this happens it will probably pay to feather the line in order to quieten down the entry.

Because bites can come so quickly, swingtips can offer a distinct advantage over bobbins because they allow a faster rod set-up – messing about with bobbins may result in missing those instant bites. Unfortunately, while feeders can produce hectic periods of activity, often these do not last long before all goes quiet again; however, it may be possible to catch at least as many tench during these mad spells, as would be likely with other methods.

Feeders are not limited to use on a paternoster. Many of those who advocate feeders prefer to incorporate them on a free-running casting boom, such as those marketed by John Roberts or Kevin Nash. This useful little tackle item will very neatly hold the hooklink clear of the feeder during casting to help prevent it spinning around the link and causing numerous tangles (Diagram 30).

Over the last few seasons I have experimented with various fixed feeder approaches in order to facilitate self-hooking. Most feeder manufacturers now make feeder systems onto which you can clip extra weight to help them hold out against the current in rivers. By coincidence this also makes them suitable for self-hooking

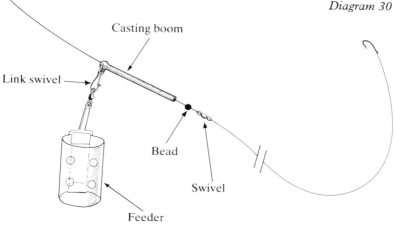

Diagram 30 Feeder on casting boom

Casting boom

Link swivel

Bead

Swivel

Feeder

Diagram 31 Fixed feeder rig

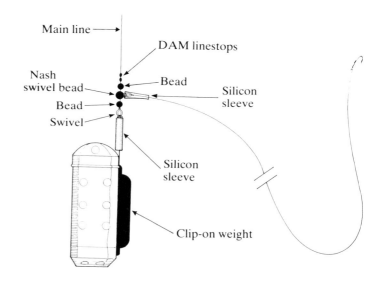

Main line

DAM linestops

Nash
swivel bead

Bead

Silicon
sleeve

Bead

Swivel

Silicon
sleeve

Clip-on weight

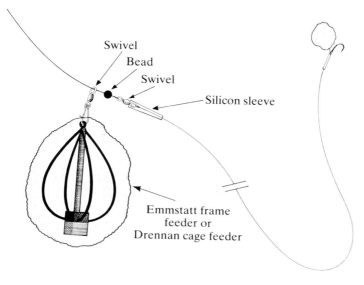

Swivel

Bead

Swivel

Silicon sleeve

Emmstatt frame
feeder or
Drennan cage feeder

Diagram 32 Cupping rig

rigs, by making them heavy enough to use to set the hook. Both open-ends and block-ends can be used successfully providing they incorporate enough lead, and I would advise using a helicopter-type rig for best results (Diagram 31).

CUPPING

Before the swimfeeders arrived, anglers used to squeeze groundbait onto the leger before casting. This method is known as cupping and has faded from popularity these days, but someone, somewhere, must still use it, as there is a little tackle item on the market known as the Emmstat Frame Feeder which is specifically designed for the job (Diagram 32). In recent seasons, I have rarely used groundbait of any sort for tench fishing, except for plugging feeders or occasionally for binding particles to be catapulted out. In most respects there seems to be few uses for cupping which cannot be better achieved with a feeder. However, cupping still has an advantage when fishing paste baits.

It is the opinion of a few fine anglers that one of the best ways of fishing pastes or boilies is to present the hookbait over a groundbait made of the same base ingredients. Certainly this will allow a quick release of attractive flavours around the hookbaits, yet it runs little chance of overfeeding the tench. Pete Springate has taken very big tench from Wraysbury using this approach. One obviously useful method of getting the groundbait out is by cupping it onto a Frame Feeder, which will allow spot-on accuracy in presentation.

Most paste ingredients will need a little doctoring to help them break down more quickly than they otherwise would. This is best achieved by mixing the dry bait mix with a quantity of brown breadcrumb, which will stop it becoming too sticky when the water is added. After casting it should break up quickly, not necessarily into a cloud, but enough to prevent it lying on the bottom in a solid mass.

Should you decide to try this method, you will probably be the only person on the water using it. Time after time, doing something different has proved to be the key to success in angling. The anglers who catch consistently are those who experiment and break new ground, initiating the fads that others copy.

5

BAIT

Principles and Application

There is a growing tendency for anglers to make bait into a very complex issue in an effort to gain that special edge. True, exceptional catches have been taken using new baits that the fish have not learned to suspect, but is this search for ultimate baits always necessary or even wise? Certainly in some waters, the tench will eat new baits readily, but in others these baits will not even be recognised as edible. Why should this happen? It is a question which bears investigation in order to understand how best to apply our baits to different waters.

A general appraisal of tench behaviour reveals that their acceptance of baits is determined by the availability of natural food, balanced against the quantity of baits they are used to encountering. In waters seldom subjected to fishing pressure, the tench will be preoccupied with the food items naturally existing in that environment. In big fish waters there is plenty of natural food available to promote rapid growth, and this abundance can condition the response of the fish – or more likely, lack of response – to baits.

In waters crammed full of natural food it may be of benefit to pre-bait regularly in order to 'break into' this feeding pattern. The intention is that the fish will eventually incorporate our offerings into their regular diet. At the other extreme, in 'pressured' waters, the tench have been fed so many different baits that they tend to feed on anything we care to throw in.

Waters are likely to vary between these opposites, and recognising where a water fits into this pattern is the starting point upon which to base any baiting approach. For example, in a virgin water where the fish have grown big on a natural larder of daphnia, snails, bloodworm and shrimps, it would be pointless to go straight in with a complex boilie, simply because such a bait would not easily fit into the fishes' conditioned style of feeding. However, a wriggling carpet of maggots, because it simulates their natural food situation, would more easily and acceptably slot into their conditioning.

This problem of conditioning can arise regularly in big tench fishing, and is evident to varying degrees both from one water to another and from one month to the next.

The Railway Lake, a hard but occasionally rewarding water

Take Wilstone, for instance. Throughout most summers the water teems with an abundance of food – the tench hardly have to work for a meal, they simply drift around and breathe it in. And according to its regulars there is no lack of fish in the water, either. Nevertheless, anglers have to struggle for a bite week in, week out. Occasionally it would seem that the profusion of this natural larder flags, then the fish are obliged to look harder to find a meal. Suddenly, anglers' baits become more attractive and some staggering catches can be made. This happens to a certain degree in most waters, and explains why tench often become difficult to catch between mid-July and September, when the natural larder is at a peak.

In other big tench waters – gravel pits especially – this situation is less apparent, perhaps because low fish density is the underlying factor behind growth rather than the richness of the water. This probably explains why boilies tend to be more instantly acceptable to pit tench.

In order better to understand our baits, it is useful to identify the principles underlying their application. Carp anglers divide baiting principles into three basic groups:

1 Natural baits: these include worms, slugs, mussels, etc.
2 Particles and mass baits: these can be further divided into two groups depending on their size. The larger items such as sweetcorn, maple peas and so on, come under the collective title of particles, while the smaller items, such as maggots and hemp, are mass baits.
3 Specials: this term usually refers to specially mixed baits such as pastes and boilies. For convenience I will include commercially available products such as bread and luncheon meat.

In practice these principles can be combined in a variety of different ways. For example, small boilies can be introduced in large quantities, so that in effect they act as particles.

NATURALS

Other than by introducing large beds of bloodworm or snails, it is doubtful if we can create effectively a natural food situation by using natural baits. Take freshwater mussels, for instance. While it would be possible for big tench to pick up small young mussels and crush them in their pharyngeal teeth, or to strip the exposed flesh from the open shell of a dead one, neither of these options provides us with a practical way of using them as bait. Another example would be with earthworms. While occasionally they may fall into the water, I doubt they feature regularly in the everyday diet of tench. Therefore the fact that these baits are natural may not be of any great significance to their appeal. Nevertheless, they still make good baits.

(top) *One of my proudest captures, a 7lb 3oz male tench*
(below) *Jim Bigden displays a beautiful beastie of 8lb 13oz*

The 'bait-munching-end' of two big tench

Earthworms, as even the most stupid schoolboy knows, are brilliant baits. Tench love them. My own preference is for lobworms and redworms. Lobs can be best acquired by collecting them off a lawn, after dark, on mild damp nights, and they can be stored in a wormery full of a mixture of soil, leaf mould and damp newspaper. On a good night, thousands of lobs can be collected by weak torchlight, but it is back-breaking work. Redworms are an easier proposition, provided you have access to well rotted horse manure or a garden compost heap.

Lobworms have acquired a very high status amongst specimen anglers, who bait them in a system known as 'the thousand lobworm trick'. As its name implies, about a thousand lobs are collected, chopped into pieces, and scattered into the swim. Then a whole lobworm is put on each rod, hooked once in the middle. This messy business is a deadly method on any tench water, and is equally effective with carp or bream.

Obviously worms don't have to be used in such vast quantities to be useful baits, although smaller amounts cannot be expected to entice large numbers of fish. As stalking baits, lobs are brilliant. Likewise, if you have exactly pinpointed fish activity, perhaps when they are patrolling a marginal weedbed prior to spawning, a single lobworm, air-injected and popped up inches off the bottom, can prove deadly for picking off passing fish. Worms also rate as perhaps the very best bait for casting to bubbling tench rooting in silt. Possibly they are mistaken for one of the natural species of freshwater worm.

Freshwater mussels are a bait which tench seem to adore, whether they occur naturally in a water or not. They can be collected quite quickly and easily from the silty margins of most 'old' waters. Open them by inserting a sharp knife into the back of the shell and then cutting the hinges which clamp the two halves together. Then cut the flesh into 3/4 in pieces, saving the firm orange parts for hookbaits and using the rest as feed.

While mussels may be an old-fashioned bait, never discount their potential: they are superb tench-catchers.

PARTICLES AND MASS BAITS

For the majority of anglers, collecting natural baits has become a thing of the past; nowadays they rely on supermarkets and tackle shops to provide easily acquired alternatives.

Of all the commercially available baits, maggots are the nation's number one favourite. In tench fishing the situation is no different – and why should it be, when you look at the vast number of big tench falling to maggots every season?

Maggots possibly come closer than any bait to mimicking a natural food situation; as a wriggling mass on the lake bed, they are totally irresisitible. Unfortunately they also attract the unwanted attention of small fish, but nonetheless, where their use is practical, they can still regularly outfish all other tench baits.

As with most mass baits, however, they may create almost as many problems as answers by being rather difficult to present as hookbaits. Early season or 'naive' tench may be prepared to accept maggots bunched on a sizeable hook, but such clumsy presentations usually prove inadequate. Soon enough, churners turn to half-hearted pulls, and takes eventually diminish into impossible twitches.

Match men will tell you that the answer is to scale down to tiny hooks and gossamer lines so that the fish cannot discriminate between the hookbait and the free offerings. With a finely dotted float this option may well fool the tench, but playing big fish on light gear is not for the faint-hearted. If you take your time it can be viable in open water, but where weedgrowth is established, it would be folly even to entertain the idea.

I have caught plenty of tench on maggots, and seldom experience too many problems while the fish are naive; but once twitches begin I am unable to recommend a totally failsafe solution, apart from jumping up and down on your rods.

It is not that there are no answers to these problems, only that there isn't a complete one. We have already discussed the underlying reasons; however, besides using short hooklinks to deal with them, there is one trick which may help in overcoming these problems. This is to mix a variety of different mass baits with a volume of larger particles. A typical mix would be one part of hemp, two parts of maggots, one part of casters, one of tares, one of sweetcorn and so on. The intention is to attempt to

Alan Wilson with his ex-record tench of 12lb 8oz taken on sweetcorn

break down some of the preoccupied grazing which mass baits create, and to fool the fish into giving better bites.

By using the larger items as hookbaits we can expect them to be picked up more readily; also, the fish will find it more difficult to discriminate between the hookbaits and free offerings, due to the confusion created by the different weights and shapes of each bait item. Thus we can hope the tench will hang on to the bait long enough to give a decent bite.

This approach is not failsafe, as tench sometimes show a tendency to discriminate and feed on one of the baits to the exclusion of the others.

Many anglers swear that casters constitute the ultimate tench bait. They are a fine proposition when they can be fed little and often, but they are very expensive and therefore unsuitable for large baitings. Also they are difficult to keep fresh during long sessions. However, there is another option for the thrifty, who might consider mixing a percentage of them with maggots and baiting the hooks with casters alone, in the hope that the fish may choose to pick up these.

Hemp is another mass bait which has universal appeal. I used to have reservations about its use for tench, but experimentation has proved that it has the same hypnotic effect on them as on roach, barbel and carp. However, the problem of impossible twitches is greater with hemp than with any other bait.

Despite the various problems mentioned here, mass baits are nonetheless superb tench catchers. In fact, I am so confident in their ability to draw and hold fish that I often introduce a quantity of them, no matter what hookbait I am using.

I have no reservations about stewed wheat. After using it for nearly thirty years it has proved its value time after time, both as a hookbait and as a versatile feed. It doesn't seem to command quite the same hypnotic appeal of most mass baits, but this can be an advantage in that it is less likely to create total preoccupation. This makes it especially useful as a feed over which to present larger offerings such as boilies.

Particles such as maggots and wheat have been used by tench anglers for many generations. In the 1970s the principles of particle bait application were developed by Rod Hutchinson and other carp angling pioneers, but in tench and barbel fishing the underlying principle has always been exploited. The idea is that the more individual food items a fish picks up, the more likely it is to lose its caution before it encounters the hookbait. Rod maintained that the more quickly a particle works, the shorter its productive life is likely to be. However, mass baits tend to have an infinitely longer active life than larger particles, simply because they so perfectly mimic the abundance of a natural larder.

One bait which constantly challenges this assertion is sweetcorn. Tench absolutely love the stuff, even when they become aware of the dangers of eating it.

Although many anglers continue to maintain that sweetcorn 'blew out' years ago on their waters, this is usually far from true. As soon as a bait fails to produce, they seem to assume that it has 'blown' once and for all, and then run around in futile effort trying to find answers for problems which do not in fact exist, changing rigs and baits until a fish is eventually caught. Once this happens, the new bait or rig is given the accolade and everything else is rejected henceforth.

I would be the last to deny that baits can have a limited effective life; but very often their failure has nothing to do with 'blowing'. Often it is merely due to the fact that the fish are not feeding, or are otherwise preoccupied in an explosion of natural food.

Even if a bait does stop producing due to excessive use, the memory of its danger will fade given time. Whilst out of favour, few anglers will use it, but eventually someone gives it another go and has a field day. And sweetcorn, providing it isn't constantly chucked in by the world and his wife, is still an exceptional tench bait. In fact, only a couple of seasons ago, on one of the most 'pressured' waters I know, it was responsible for numerous big tench and far more carp than any of the ultra-modern baits in use.

In fact particles seldom 'blow out' in the way most anglers understand it. I remember the astonishment of one angler who took his dinghy out to inspect his swim, only to find that all the bait he had put out previously had gone; all that remained were his three baited hooks.

This probably occurs more often than we would care to believe. Clearly the fish still *want* the bait, but they can obviously reject the hookbaits. Now, I don't pretend that the following suggestion would necessarily be the best strategy. However, it is possible that by neutralising the weight of the hook with a little polystyrene, you will outwit a cautious fish or two.

The list of effective particles must be endless: black eye beans, haricot beans, chick peas, maple peas, tic beans and yellow peas, all have an impressive track record. One angler I know even had fair results using tiger nuts and peanuts, though when using them for carp, I have yet to catch a tench instead.

All particles must be thoroughly soaked before use, and most require cooking. In my experience they have a greater appeal with tench if cooked a little softer than when preparing them for carp.

Most particles can take flavours and dye, either to make them more attractive, or to disguise them after catches start to wane. Flavouring can be achieved easily, after cooking, by soaking them in a dilution of artificial flavouring, or simply by spraying them in a plastic bag with an atomiser marketed by Richworths. Another useful dodge is to boil them up in a powdered soup.

Black eyes, haricots and chick peas are ideal for flavouring and I would suggest using 10ml of flavour per pound of prepared bait. Maples and tic beans can be flavoured, though I doubt there is a more effective method of preparing them than allowing them to ferment. The resulting mess will stink horribly but although this may put you off, the tench will love it!

It is certainly the volume of bait which makes particles such effective fish-catchers, but this in itself can present tench anglers with a dilemma – namely how much to put in without overdoing it. When fishing close in or baiting with swimfeeders, a steady, regular feeding pattern is easy to maintain. However, once the tench really get their heads down, they can quickly eat a lot of bait, so it pays to get several large pouch-fuls out to start with.

Baiting with particles at longer distances is a time-honoured problem and many methods have been developed to get them out. Mixing the bait with breadcrumb and catapulting balls of it out can be as good a way as any, up to a distance of about 60 yards; but when fishing long sessions of a few days or more, I prefer to use a dinghy. Boats allow unrivalled accuracy; and providing you use them carefully and quietly, they have a minimal effect on fish. In fact, when baiting from a dinghy, I have seen tench roll right alongside and have even picked them up on the sonar as they were feeding actively on the bait down below.

Nonetheless, there are problems in using boats on many waters. On some, they are banned outright; on others, you must be careful not to upset other anglers.

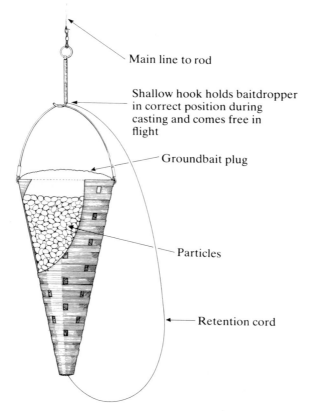

Main line to rod

Shallow hook holds baitdropper in correct position during casting and comes free in flight

Groundbait plug

Particles

Retention cord

Diagram 33 Baitdropper (cut-away view)

Another thought worthy of consideration is how much you value your life: cheap inflatable dinghies have a habit of splitting at the seams – should this happen 80 yards out you may find yourself immersed in deep and cold water. So don't take risks: if you do a fair amount of baiting from a dinghy, it will be worth investing in one of the small fibreglass models which will fit neatly onto a car roof-rack and will afford a far greater measure of safety.

Baitdroppers are very popular and are sold in most good tackle shops. However, they are awkward to cast accurately, most are noisy, and few are suited for use with smaller particles, such as hemp. The only one I like was designed by Coventry specimen hunter Merv Wilkinson and is marketed by Gordon Griffiss.

This ingenious model (Diagram 33) is rather like a small cone-shaped bucket, tied onto the line by a link leading from its pointed end. After filling, the particles are packed in with a small amount of breadcrumb. Before casting, the little handle-like catch on top of the dropper is hung onto a shallow hook on the other end of the link; this prevents the dropper unloading its cargo during casting. In flight, the dropper is released from the hook and becomes free to travel aerodynamically to its destination. Just before touchdown, it is possible to jerk-stop the dropper, making it spray its load onto the target area. This allows the dropper to land fairly quietly on the water, before being reeled in across the surface.

SPECIALS

'Specials' is a term usually used to describe baits specially made up by anglers. For convenience, however, I will include many shop-bought products which can be used successfully as bait. The most well known and underrated of all these is good old-fashioned bread. It is remarkable that bread ever lost its place as a top tench bait as it can give any other bait a run for its money. Its taste and texture are unique, it is easily seen, and it can rest delicately on top of weed and silt, all of which add greatly to its use and attraction.

One time-honoured dodge is to use a carpet of mashed bread with a hookbait of flake; but in fact flake can be effective when used as a single offering without any groundbait whatsoever. Many years ago, on Johnson's Lakes, angling cartoonist Cliff Hatton demonstrated the viability of this approach. He sat in the swim next to mine alongside his fishing partner; they were using two rods each, all baited with flake, and cast to a useful but unbaited patrolling area. As I watched them wind in a succession of good fish, I was nonplussed, particularly as my expensive carpet of maggots, wheat and sweetcorn placed along a normally productive drop-off, failed to produce a single bite. Since that day I have often used a third rod baited with flake to explore areas other than my baited one, with great success.

For bread flake, a loaf of medium-sliced white bread is ideal. Simply pull off a large enough piece to wrap once around the inside of the hook shank, then pinch it on, leaving the point exposed. The way it settles on top of a weedbed cannot be bettered by any other bait. It is possible to flavour flake in order to gain an advantage and this has worked well in the past; but flake tends to be so rarely used by other anglers in recent years, that this practice is probably unnecessary.

Breadcrust provides us with a hassle-free pop-up which also takes some beating. I prefer the crust from an unsliced 'tin' loaf, which is neither too hard nor too soft. Before baiting the hook, I cut the crust into bait-sized pieces with scissors, which avoids squeezing out any of its natural buoyancy.

Being so buoyant, crust can be a useful medium for balancing other baits. For example, a tiny piece put on a small hook with a single maggot or grain of sweetcorn will help neutralise the weight of the hook, thus making it more acceptable to suspicious fish.

Luncheon meat is another supermarket product which is easy to use and has taken many big tench over the years; however, it is now rarely employed. It can be presented as large cubes, or be chopped into tiny particles. There are several brands on the market; some are dense and meaty, while others have a high fat content which makes them almost neutral in buoyancy and therefore ideal for fishing in silt or weed. My own favourites are 'bacon grill' and 'chopped pork with ham' – unfortunately these also happen to be rather expensive.

MODERN SPECIALS, PASTES AND BOILIES

Luncheon meat and pork sausage meat can be mashed and mixed with breadcrumb, sausage rusk or a combination of modern boilie ingredients. Potentially this offers a tremendous variety of different meat paste baits.

Pastes can be presented on the hook, but another way – my preference – is to mould them onto a Roberts' bead tied to the end of a short hair rig. Another dodge to give buoyancy to pastes is to use a little polyball instead of a bead on the hair.

During the seventies and early eighties, tench baits were dragged slowly out of the confines of traditional practice largely as a result of the numbers of tench falling

One of my early successes with boilies. This one weighed 7lb 13oz

to carp anglers' boilies and paste baits. Many of us started experimenting by using these specifically for tench, and a whole world of possibilities opened up ...

I suppose for many of us, these developments began with trout pellet pastes. Trout pellets are proven fish-catchers which, once again, are usually overlooked by anglers who prefer to follow only the latest fashionable bait trends. They can be made into a paste easily by soaking them in boiling water, then mashing them up until the required consistency is achieved. If necessary, the resulting paste can be stiffened up with a few ounces of semolina.

Trout pellets have the reputation of possessing instant appeal. Nevertheless most pastes and boilies benefit from a certain amount of pre-baiting to get them established. How long it will take to get the fish on the bait depends on a variety of factors already discussed (see p68); though it is noticeable that while some baits incite an instant response, others need time to work, but in the long run could prove far superior.

There is a vast range of different bait ingredients, including various powders, meals, compounds, extracts, enzymes, oils and synthetic flavours; these are now available from tackle shops and mail order companies. The following list includes a large proportion of these ingredients. Many are proven fish-catchers; others are worthy of experimentation. While most carp anglers will be well versed in using them, the majority of tench anglers will probably have only a limited knowledge, so I hope the following may serve as a useful introduction.

Milk derivatives include:
Casein, very popular as a major ingredient in HNV baits; 80 mesh casein is best for making softer baits and is therefore better suited to tench fishing.
Calcium caseinate, a protein-rich soluble version of lactic casein.
Sodium caseinate, an extremely light protein-rich version of soluble caseinate, which adds buoyancy to a bait.
Lactalbumen, a high protein milk by-product.
Lactalpro, a low protein milk powder, ideal for carrying flavours in attracter baits.
Vitamealo, another low protein milk product, with a very creamy flavour, also useful in attracter baits.

Soya products include:
Soya isolate, the isolated protein of soya beans, a useful HNV ingredient.
50% protein soya flour, ideal for carrying flavours in attracter baits.
Full fat soya flour, oil-rich, cheap and ideal for carrying flavours.

Fish meals include:
White fish meal, a real winner, tench love it.
Herring meal, mackerel meal, sardine meal, sand eel meal, capelin meal and anchovy meal, all proven tench-catchers.

Tuna meal and red fish meal, untried by me but obviously well worth experimenting with.

Shrimp meal, very buoyant so use no more than 2oz in a mix. It needs grinding for best results.

Codlivine, a fish-derived vitamin supplement; it has a good reputation with tench fishermen.

Animal product meals include:

Meat and bone meal, a very useful ingredient but needs sifting to enable easy bait-rolling.

Blood albumen, a water-soluble protein which unfortunately is hard to get but is deadly in meaty mixes.

Liver powder, superb in amounts of up to 2oz per mix.

Meat protein, blood plasma, blood meal and red cells, all recent products produced by Cotswold Baits. They are untried by me, but are obvious candidates for experimentation.

Vegetable meals include:

Molasses meal, a highly recommended product with a strong distinctive flavour.

Hemp meal; all cyprinids love hemp.

Roast peanut meal, a tasty nutritious addition to various baits.

Roast hazelnut meal, same as above.

Wheatgerm, a useful addition to any sweet bait.

Semolina, a useful ingredient to enable easy mixing and bulking out. Also for carrying flavours in attracter baits.

Wheat gluten, an essential binding agent. Use 1oz in most 10oz mixes and up to 2oz in fish meals.

Birdfood and seed mixes:

Robin Red, a red, spicy birdfood, beloved by carp anglers and which has accounted for many tench captures.

Sluice, another highly recommended birdfood which combines well and is easy to roll.

Nectarblend, a popular ingredient used in combination with other birdfoods.
    PTX, same as above.

Budgie protein food, useful for boosting protein levels of birdfood baits.

Miscellaneous ingredients:

Blue cheese powder and orange cheese powder, tasty and nutritional additions to numerous recipes. Available from Cotswold Baits.

Daphnia meal, very expensive but a little goes a long way. Available from Premier Baits.

Bloodworm meal, costs more than gold dust, but could undoubtedly be worth the
  expense. Also available from Premier Baits.
Trout pellets, a very nutritious commercial trout feed.
Trout fry crumb, a crumbled trout feed, an excellent ingredient.
Ground dog or cat biscuits, very useful and cheap, the meatier the better.
Egg albumen, a water-soluble high protein product derived from eggs and useful in
  HNV baits.
Egg replacer, used as an alternative to eggs to mix in with boilie ingredients.

For those not keen to experiment in developing their own mixes, there is a large
range of ready-mixed paste and boilie base mixes available. The 'Catchum' range of
pre-packed pastes, originally designed by Rod Hutchinson, have proved particularly
effective tench baits. The Seafood Blend is especially good, with Extract Blend and
Minglefruit following close behind. When using these or any paste recipes of your
own, mix them with lake water, as there are so many chemicals in our tap-water
which could possibly taint and spoil what would otherwise be a winning bait.

Boilies were originally created in an effort to overcome the problem of small fish
whittling down paste baits. Their greater resilience is achieved by mixing the bait
ingredients with eggs; after rolling into individual baits they are then boiled to make
them hard. This process solves a multitude of baiting problems: being round, they
are perfect for catapulting to distances previously impossible to reach with other
baits; and being hard, they do not break down in the water.

Before the development of boilies, anglers had concerned themselves only with
the taste of a bait; however, Fred Wilton's revolutionary high protein theory soon
turned all that on its head. He maintained that by using a bait which fulfilled all a
fish's dietary requirements, and once it had had time to establish itself, it would be
eaten in preference to any other available food source. It took the angling world a
while to come to terms with this development, but no one could deny the fact that
Fred and his followers were catching an unprecedented number of carp.

Fred's high protein – or more correctly, 'High Nutritional Value' ('HNV') baits –
were developed until eventually they were made from only the finest milk protein
products. Fred insisted that the flavour was of no importance whatsoever, its only
function being to provide a label by which the fish would recognise the bait. In fact
the flavour levels of HNVs are usually kept low so as not to overstate the taste, for it
is likely that strong flavours will 'blow' the bait more quickly. HNV recognition
relies on a significant amount of pre-baiting so the fish become conditioned to the
bait's food value, and will keep looking for more.

At risk of being challenged by Fred – and he is a big man! – I do believe that
although HNV baits will work as well with tench as they do with carp, there is actually no advantage in using them unless you intend to put a lot of fishing effort into
the chosen water.

If this is not your intention, it is possible to make cheaper baits simply by boosting flavour levels; these will have more instant appeal, even though they are made of ingredients which offer little food value. They are known as 'attracter' or 'carrier' baits. In theory, they are unlikely to have the same effective life-span that nutritional baits offer; in practice, however, this is not always the case.

Just how long it will take to establish an HNV bait is open to debate. Some recipes have a more instant appeal than others. Again in theory, once the fish are on a good HNV, results should improve with use.

The following recipes have proved useful. For further information I would recommend that you read the bait chapters in Kevin Maddocks' book *Carp Fever*. A typical HNV bait is usually made up in 10oz mixes, from various milk protein products, added to four medium-sized eggs. Protein levels would be around 80 per cent plus. The following recipe is a good example with a proven track record.

HNV Milk Protein Mix

4oz 80 mesh casein
2oz calcium caseinate
1oz lactalbumen
1oz soya isolate

1oz wheat gluten
1oz Equivite or Vitrex
3–5ml of liquid flavour

For more buoyant baits, replace calcium caseinate with 2oz of sodium caseinate.

Carp anglers tend to boil their baits until rock hard. Tench, however, most definitely prefer softer baits, so a boiling time of about 30 seconds should be sufficient, long enough to skin them while letting them remain quite soft inside. They will require a longer drying period, though, before bagging up, otherwise they tend to get mis-shapen.

In attracter or carrier baits, taste and smell are all-important so the flavour levels are usually quite high. Be careful though! *Too* much flavour will repel the fish and thus spoil the effect of the bait. The following recipe is a typical example of one of these baits.

Attracter or Flavour-Carrier Bait

5oz semolina
3oz full fat soya flour
1oz Lactalpro
5–10ml liquid flavour

1oz wheat gluten
5ml intense sweetener, used in
   dairy or fruity baits
1 teaspoon flavour enhancer

The range of bait mixes and ingredients available on the market grows larger each season, and in general the quality is very good. However many ingredients, especially milk proteins, have a very short shelf-life; not many companies use sell-by dates, so make sure that the goods haven't spent months or even years in storage.

What are the best flavours for baits? This is almost impossible to answer as tench will accept a vast variety of tastes – in fact, I have yet to find a flavour they will not accept. Nevertheless, a few have stood out consistently over the years. Tutti-frutti, Topper, strawberry, Scopex and banana for instance, are all reliable fruity flavours which tend to have instant appeal and benefit from being used together with a sweetener. Chocolate malt, maple, maple cream and condensed milk have been just as good, and amongst the savoury flavours boiled ham, and pukka salmon and seafood are all very effective. Bun spice and ultra-spice also take honours.

Bulk oils, essential oils, amino acids, appetite-stimulators and flavour-enhancers can also be used to enhance the individuality and effectiveness of a bait. However, take care when you use these products, as successful application of many of them requires that you follow the manufacturers' guidelines exactly. They have been field-tested to establish the most effective level required, and to exceed these measures could well be positively disadvantageous.

As an alternative to milk products, fish and meat meals can be used to make some very effective and nutritional baits. The following recipes have proved to be very reliable and although they can show instant results, they benefit greatly from pre-baiting.

Fish Meal Boilie

3oz casein
2oz white fish meal
2oz sand eel meal
1oz mackerel meal
1oz shrimp meal

1oz wheat gluten
1ml blended fish oil
2ml emulsifier
5ml seafood liquid flavour

Meat Meal Boilie

3oz blood albumen
3oz meat and bone meal
1oz liver powder
2oz 80 mesh casein

1oz wheat gluten
1 teaspoon multi-flavour enhancer
5ml meaty or spicy flavour

Fish and meat meals can be rather difficult to roll into baits and are therefore often better mixed with other types of ingredient. For example, 4 or 5oz of milk proteins would greatly aid rolling and might also make a more individual and palatable bait.

By mixing different types of ingredients like this we may be moving away from a strictly high protein concept. However protein levels, and how high they need to be, provoke constant debate. In fact many very successful anglers deny the importance of high protein levels altogether, especially in the summer – that is, tench-fishing time – when despite all our theorising the fish seem just as happy to eat baits containing lower protein levels. Therefore, we could expect baits with protein levels of only 40 to 50 per cent, but incorporating a good taste, to prove just as effective during the summer as a proper HNV bait. I therefore offer these two recipes as perfectly acceptable:

2oz white fish meal
2oz sardine meal
1oz capelin meal
2oz Sluice 'CLO' birdfood
2oz casein
1oz lactalbumin
30ml cod liver oil
1ml sweetener
5ml flavour

3oz Sluice 'CLO' birdfood
2oz Robin Red birdfood
2oz casein
1oz lactalbumin
1oz sand eel meal
1oz wholewheat semolina
2ml sweetener
5ml ultra spice flavour

Boilies can be rolled into various sizes, depending on how you intend to use them. At a standard 14 to 16mm they provide us with a versatile bait which can be catapulted accurately up to 70 yards. Larger baits will catapult further and can also be used selectively as they are more likely to pick up only bigger fish. Mini-boilies of 6 to 10mm tend to attract roach and bream, but are perfect for use as particles thus combining the concepts of nutrition and preoccupation through availability.

Nowadays the shops are piled high with a multitude of ready-made frozen or shelf-life boilies; Richworth's Stream Select, for example, market a huge range of shelf-life boilies, and these are very useful when fishing long sessions on distant waters, since it is difficult to keep baits fresh for such long periods of time. They are produced in 18 and 10mm sizes and in a large range of flavours; many of these have proved effective – particularly the tutti-frutti, tropicano, bird food and strawberry yoghurt – and they have the advantage of being fairly soft, especially when they have been in the water for a while.

Richworth also produce a fair range of frozen pre-packed boilies, which in many ways are nicer baits than the shelf-lives. Because they do not dissolve slowly as is the case with some shelf-life baits, they are more likely still to be on the hook the following morning. The tutti-frutti, salmon supreme, boiled ham and strawberry cream frozen baits are all proven tench-catchers. Moreover the Richworth range of frozen pre-packed mini-boilies make perfect particles.

Boilies are not the ultimate bait. They are just one of many options open to us, each of which will work in the right circumstances. Many anglers seem to delight in denigrating them as tench bait, though this may be because they fail to understand the basic principles involved in them. For my part, they have provided a very effective, convenient and totally versatile approach to tench fishing, and have led to the capture of very many good fish. They are not necessarily the best choice of bait on all waters or at all times. However, I now rely on them for at least 50 per cent of my tench fishing, and without them would consider my bait repertoire very limited indeed.

CEREAL GROUNDBAITING

Over the last ten years or so the practice of cereal groundbaiting in big tench fishing has been gradually superseded by the swimfeeder and more recently by boilies. On top of this, many specialist anglers have taken to using a dinghy or model boat to get their feed where they want it, resulting in its further decline.

This situation is hardly surprising when you consider that baiting with pinpoint accuracy has become progressively more important with the development of feature fishing on gravel pits. At any great distance the introduction of groundbait balls to particular features is likely to be a rather hit-or-miss affair. For most of us, long-range groundbaiting is an art which can take a good while to master, and 60 yards or so is about as far as we could hope to manage with any accuracy.

Nonetheless cereal groundbaiting will always have a place in tench fishing; despite its shortcomings, it still offers possibilities too valuable to overlook. Therefore an understanding of its use will always be of benefit.

The principle of cereal groundbait is to bind up items of loose feed into balls so they can be projected to distances otherwise unattainable. However, this is not the

An 8lb 7oz which I took by fishing boilies over a bed of wheat

limit of its use, because it can be equally viable as an attracter in its own right; though special ingredients or flavours will need to be added so as to strengthen its appeal. And you can always incorporate these two elements by making a highly attractive groundbait which is also used to bind items of loose feed.

Many specimen anglers of the younger generation seem to have no idea about using cereal groundbaits, so a look at its basic application might be helpful.

Ideally, groundbait should be mixed on the dry side, its consistency loose enough for it to break up and disperse in the water, rather than so sticky that it lies on the bottom as a fish-filling stodge. The idea is that it should attract the fish and keep them searching for food, rather than filling them up. In practice however, it may have to be more of a compromise. For example, a dry, soft ball of feed cannot be expected to hold together when projected over excessive distances; the necessary ferocity of its launch from the catapult would simply cause it to disintegrate in mid-flight.

Ideally, groundbait should hold together after launching until it splashes down. The impact should split the ball and start it breaking up, so that it disintegrates and releases its contents on the way to the bottom. In practice this may prove a tall order, but it can be done provided the consistency of the mix is right. If you follow the simple method described here, it should help to achieve the right consistency.

1 Always mix groundbait in a shallow bowl, never in a bucket; it is impossible to achieve an even mix right down to the bottom of a bucket.

2 Use brown breadcrumb as the main ingredient of all stillwater groundbaits. It is less sticky, and so less likely to mix up too stiff to break down quickly in the water. If it won't hold together for long-distance work, a percentage of white breadcrumb will help bind it up.

3 Use lake water to mix with the groundbait. Be sparing with the water, a little goes a long way, and always put it in the bowl first and then add the crumb to it, a little at a time.

   Once the consistency is right, you should be able to mould it into balls without too much trouble (it is better if you wet your hands first) – when crushed, the ball should break apart and crumble in your hands quite easily.

4 Do not mix up too much groundbait at a time; as the crumb absorbs the moisture and slowly dries out, it will become rather unmanageable and require the addition of more water. While you can get away with this soon after mixing, after an hour or two it becomes more difficult to get the consistency right.

5 Try mixing a ball and throwing it down into the margins, where you can watch it and get some idea of how quickly it is breaking down in the water. You can also get a good idea of how well the mix is behaving by paying attention to its entry into the water after you catapult it out. Groundbait of the correct consistency will make a considerably less noisy splash, simply because it will burst upon impact. If you look carefully, you should be able to see if the ball breaks up properly as the

splash should carry a suspension of groundbait particles which will colour it up. Get it right and the splash will be brown; make it too stiff and it will be clear.

Whenever using groundbait to project baits such as sweetcorn or hemp, I like to add the liquid from the bait to the mix, which I am sure helps make the groundbait more attractive.

It is surprising just how much feed can be packed into the groundbait, but avoid overdoing it. This will only make it more difficult to bind and probably result in the balls breaking up in mid-flight, scattering bait all over the place.

There are all manner of ingredients which can be added to make the groundbait more attractive; look back through the special ingredients used for making pastes and boilies where you will find a variety of meals and powders to experiment with: various fish meals, meat and bone meal or various blood compounds; hemp meal, though this is not as effective as cooked hemp; also molasses meal, layers' mash, ground trout pellets or salmon fry crumb, all proven winners.

For close-range work a groundbait mix may require about 40–50 per cent of brown crumb to prevent the ingredients getting too sticky. However, long-range work may need something a little bit more glutinous for binding; perhaps replace some of the brown crumb with a similar quantity of white.

Water-soluble flavours can prove to be an invaluable addition to all groundbaits; the list of viable flavours is endless, and I have no doubt that at times they can make the difference between catching or blanking. I would recommend using flavours at a level of around 10ml per pound of dry ingredients.

Over short distances groundbait can be thrown out by hand, but long-range work will require a decent catapult – the Drennan 'Whopper Dropper' groundbait catapult is perfect for this job. The performance of a catapult can be controlled by varying the length of its elastics, as this determines the power of the launch: longer elastics provide a softer launch which will help prevent soft balls of feed breaking up in flight; this also limits the effective range, however. Shortening the elastics increases ferocity so they will punch the feed further out, though in this case you will need to stiffen up the mix considerably if it is to survive the impact of its launch.

In my experience it is better not to make groundbait balls too large: larger balls greatly inhibit the distance which can be reached, and also tend to break up in flight more easily; a small chicken's egg is a good guide for size. Smaller balls allow greater accuracy, and make a quieter impact with the water; furthermore, if one or two smaller balls should break up in flight, there will be far less feed scattered all over the swim.

6

DIVERSE APPROACHES

Opening day, 16 June, has always been synonymous with tench-fishing for me, and since childhood I can only remember one spent in pursuit of other species. I find that early season tench-fishing has a powerful magic all of its own, which is an odd compulsion really, as early season tench can be so unpredictable. This is partly because they are so often subjected to the crazy whims of our weather, obliged to endure either a heatwave or a miserably cold spell – but even more unsettling is their annual obsession with sexual activity.

Looking back, those early season sessions when everything went right tend to stand out in one's memory; conditions were pleasant, the fish were feeding and the sacks were always wet. In actual fact though – more often that we care to admit – the tench were either spawning full-time, or otherwise so preoccupied with the idea, that feeding took a back seat. Which is hardly surprising considering their sexual activities are conducted as an annual orgy with the entire neighbourhood; it must be hard to pay due attention to eating!

Despite these problems, most big fish specialists will be hoping the fish have not spawned out, because they will then be caught at their heaviest. This may seem an unattractive philosophy, but it is inevitable in this age of chasing records or 'personal bests'; while pretty or nicely proportioned fish are always appreciated, biggest is still best, provided they are healthy and not dropsical or spawnbound. And the best tench are going to be at their biggest during the opening fortnight, when they could be carrying in excess of 1½lb of spawn.

Some anglers feel that the act of catching spawny fish must cause additional stress when they are at their most vulnerable. However, I have yet to witness the death of a single tench due to being caught 'in spawn', so can only conclude that providing we take every care to minimise stress while the fish are out of the water, they should not suffer greatly from the experience.

Tench weigh their heaviest early in the season, which is why few specialists bother to fish seriously for them once their weight drops after spawning – barbel, chub and pike weigh heavier later in the season, thus allowing a longer period in which to pursue the biggest. This is a pity, because this attitude has rather devalued tench as a major species. However, spawned-out eight- and nine-pounders are very rare indeed in all but a few exceptional waters, but because these are the target weights that big fish anglers are seeking, most will lose interest after the fish drop below this weight.

The outcome of all this is that tench – which surely deserve recognition as one of our most fascinating and challenging species – have become one of the least understood. This is undoubtedly because only a dedicated few fish for them beyond the first few weeks of the season. The pity of it is, that no matter how heavy a spawny tench may weigh, a big spawned-out specimen will always be a magnificent creature which will probably be more challenging to catch and will fight much harder. Surely this makes them well worth pursuing long after they have spawned out, even though they are unlikely to reach the weights which hit the headlines.

Despite this assertion I, too, often fail to give tench the attention they deserve after the first month or so. Early season big tench fishing for me entails travelling long distances and by mid-July I will usually have landed my fair share of biggies in the course of the fishing I have travelled away for – my passion for big tench will usually be satiated. After this effort, it is difficult to get excited about struggling for the odd five- or six-pounders from waters in my locality, particularly as there is plenty of worthwhile fishing for other species. Be that as it may, should any big tench start showing up within striking distance, I am likely to be fishing for them well beyond spawning time.

For example, the hot summers and mild winters of 1987 to 1990 appear to have prompted a large spurt of growth in the fish of a few Norfolk waters, and next summer I fully intend to launch a campaign for a Norfolk 'eight', of which only a handful have ever been caught – indeed until recently such a fish has been very rare, and generally too much of a long shot to generate a great deal of enthusiasm.

You may already have guessed that at least during the first few weeks of the tench-fishing season, I become something of a bivvie-dweller. Some anglers criticise this style of fishing, but it suits my needs perfectly by allowing me an intensive effort at a really big one. What's more it is enjoyable and as far as I can see, harms no one – unless it is those anglers (probably the same critics) who are not prepared to make the effort, but nevertheless expect to be able to walk into the productive swims whenever it suits them.

Long-stay fishing can certainly get results, but it is no guarantee of it. It can also be extremely hard work. In June the days are long, and most nights will probably bring no more than a few hours sleep, (that is, if the tench don't feed throughout the night); and when the dawn comes, the active angler will need to be up and ready. Furthermore it is at dawn that tench are most visibly active, when the watchful angler is able to learn most about their movements.

Later on there may be time to relax, but bites can be expected at least until midday and if conditions suit and you are in the right swim, activity could continue periodically throughout the day. In recent seasons however, the sun has often become too hot; and although normally this might have been a good time to catch up on a few hours' sleep, the bivvie was likely to have become unbearably sweltering.

I am not complaining: this approach to fishing is my own choice, because it

A rare sight – a 7lb 7oz Norfolk gravel-pit tench

gets the results; and you only get out of fishing what you put into it. However, there is a limit to the amount of effort anyone can put in, before effectiveness diminishes; and the more tired we become, the worse this can get until eventually it is possible to slump into total exhaustion. Then it is almost impossible to make sense of what the fish are up to, and there is little chance of responding intelligently to any given situation. Hopefully though, one's efforts will not have gone unrewarded.

Take Alan Wilson, for example: some anglers criticise him for his full-time approach to fishing – presumably because they feel they cannot compete with his efforts or hope to match his results. For my own part, there is no way I would want

Alan's life-style, but having spent some time with him, I am amazed that after years of living next to the water, this man bubbles with more enthusiasm than most of us can muster after a couple of days. And when spending more than a few days at a water, there is much that can be learnt from Alan's approach. Maybe the most important lesson is to develop a methodical approach to long-stay fishing, rather than letting enthusiasm run away with you.

To be 'methodical' sounds rather boring, as if it lacks inspiration, but it needn't be at all. It means no more than taking the time to get things sorted out step by step, so as to make the best of the various possibilities the water offers. This process starts with the swim. Why choose this one, or bait these particular areas? Why adopt a particular system, a certain type of baiting?

And what is the best choice of early season swim? Obviously, unless the tench have already spawned, it would be the areas in which they are likely to do so. On shallower waters this may not be so very critical, but on most there will be only a handful of suitable spawning sites. Once located, they can produce tench fishing of an unbelievable standard; but miss them, and the bobbins may fail to twitch for days on end.

Margin fishing is very often a good proposition for early season tench; it is also one which many anglers seem to overlook, even when the fish are visibly swimming around under their rod-tips. This lack of initiative is difficult to understand, and I can only put it down to an obsession with casting long distances; everyone apparently wants to fish the far bank margins, happily overlooking the fact that the margin under their noses may well be just as productive – *and* very much easier to bait and cast to.

I love margin fishing myself, and whenever there is enough deep water close in, I am likely either to have a hookbait in it or otherwise have it baited and under a watchful eye. Tench can be caught in the margins throughout the year, but it is during the pre-spawning period that these areas tend to come into their own.

When the fish are in close, there is the chance to enjoy what is surely the most exciting form of tench fishing; in clear water they can usually be seen cruising to and fro, sometimes alone but often in groups of four or five. This is also an ideal time to study behaviour or to watch their reactions to baits and rigs; it provides a refreshing contrast to the comparative dullness of most stillwater bottom fishing.

One of my more lasting memories is that of a 7lb 6oz tench picking up a large pinch of breadflake on a self-hooking rig which I had dropped three feet out from the bank. I know that a purist would have free-lined it or at least employed a float, but the devil in me wanted to watch a fish's reaction to picking up a bait and hooking itself. The contrast between the gentle feeding motions of that fish, and the wave of total shock that rocked through its body as it gently pulled the line tight to the lead, was a sight to be seen. When it fully grasped the gravity of its situation it powered off into the lake.

When tench move in close it may be possible to stalk them rather than sitting it out in a bivvie, and stalking can prove a very effective way of catching fish. I have already mentioned an 8lb 5oz tench I caught this way (see p32) and stalking has provided me with a few other captures which otherwise would not have come my way. When I first moved to Norfolk, the celebrated Marsh Lake had already slipped far into decline; and when I first decided to fish it early in the following summer, a number of its regulars had been bivvied up all week along the favourite bank. However, apparently they had blanked.

Rather than join in this lack of activity, I decided that a better alternative would be to visit the water as often as was practical in an attempt to locate some fish visually, before even thinking about wetting a line. Sure enough on my third visit, a scattering of tench were to be seen drifting around in the gin-clear shallows, obviously gathered there in preparation for spawning. I rushed off home to grab the rods and returned in minutes: within the following hour, two fish weighing 6lb 6oz and 5lb 14oz picked up my simple offering of link-legered breadflake. They hardly qualified for the Drennan Cup, I know; but they did represent a large percentage of the fish caught that week, which goes to show that there is sometimes more sense in the opportunistic approach, rather than blindly putting in the rod hours.

One of the obvious ways of approaching early season tench is to pre-bait a swim for a week or two before the opening. And judging by the number of signs one sees of this practice during the last weeks of the close season, it is a popular approach. For my own part, although I have launched successful pre-baiting campaigns and would not hesitate to do so again if I felt the need arise, I am seldom convinced that I would not have caught those fish anyway. And while a campaign may have worked well enough for me, other anglers on the same water often managed to catch just as many if not more fish without encumbering themselves with this laborious task.

Nevertheless, pre-baiting is always worthy of consideration. It should not be relied upon to draw fish into an area on its own, but it may be beneficial providing you first make sure that there are already tench resident in that area. This may be stating the obvious, but it is a fairly common mistake; and it cannot be overstressed that most big tench waters are sparsely populated – there will be hotspots with fish in residence, but also vast areas without any at all. However, pre-baiting barren areas is unlikely to attract them in significant numbers, while in the hotspots, pre-baiting for the sake of it may have little value because the fish are already present.

Nowadays, although I would welcome the opportunity to pre-bait in order to establish a new bait, I believe a few hours spent locating the fish will be far more worth while than all the pre-baiting in the world. For example, on one occasion a friend and I turned up at a very popular water in the very early hours on 16 June. By dawn we had located a large amount of fish activity in two swims next door to an angler who had been in residence and pre-baiting for a few days. By the end of that week we had taken a significant number of big tench and carp from those swims, while the angler in the pre-baited swim failed to get a single bite.

As mentioned earlier, tench can prove to be very fickle around spawning time, and while bites are usually big and bold, occasionally they will just twitch. In fact I doubt that this pre-spawning twitching has anything to do with caution, blown baits,

rigs, or anything else to do with fishing: it seems that the tench are merely playing with the baits, rather like someone with a poor appetite. This may well sound far-fetched, but I have seen it happen so often, and there are few other likely explanations.

This situation never lasts long, and after spawning, bites tend to become much bolder. These twitches can be dealt with by hovering over the rod and swatting at every movement of the bobbins. However, fishing a short hooklink on a fixed lead can be just as effective.

Tench are unlikely to have shed all their spawn before fishing commences. Once the temperatures become hot and settled and the water reaches about 70° Fahrenheit, they will really get down to it and you will be lucky to get any bites at all. A flick through my records of early season captures often shows gaps of a day or two when nothing was caught, when the fish were obviously spawning.

Spawning is likely to take place intermittently over several days; it is seldom completed at one time, and usually some spawning activity will carry on at least until mid-July. Once the main spawning flurry is over, the fish will start feeding in earnest and catches will begin to pick up – though your chances of breaking any records could well be over for another year.

This is when some specimen hunters give up tench fishing for the rest of the season. However, for those with a deeper appreciation of the species, the real fun begins at this time: with spawning finished, the tench will be hungry and should start feeding with abandon; the fishing is likely to be at its best and while the fish remain in the area, large catches can be taken.

By the end of July the last few females should have spawned, and as they gradually vacate the area, catches will start to drop off. The proportion of male fish caught will increase, simply because they will be reluctant to leave until the last females have been served. Then, catches from the area will diminish altogether.

At this point the tench tend to spread out and become more nomadic in nature, usually roaming and feeding over larger areas of deeper water; as a consequence the fishing becomes less hotspot orientated. Nevertheless, some spots prove consistently more productive than others, and it is not always easy to define what the fish find attractive. Presumably it is an abundance of natural food, but often there are not many obvious features to recommend these swims so you will just have to keep a watchful eye!

As summer progresses it becomes less predictable as to when fish will feed; as always, the morning will be the main period but night feeding may feature more. However, few big tench waters are very productive at night – especially pits – and generally I would be more confident of bites even during the middle of the afternoon.

By July weed growth will probably have reached horrendous proportions, making rig presentation difficult, and hooked fish taking some effort to extract. It will be tempting to get a weed-rake out to clear an open area, and indeed in some waters there may be no other option. Where weed growth is relatively sparse its removal should

Jim Bigden with an 8lb 10oz and three 6s from a spawning site swim

cause few problems, but on cleared swims and after a few weeks of angling pressure, tench can become very nervous of entering these areas. They will swim quickly through them, obviously aware of the bait but far too nervous about the lack of cover to get their heads down. Meanwhile it is often possible to pick up a fish or two in the surrounding weedy areas simply by popping the bait into small clear gaps.

Where raking is unavoidable it is best to confine it to clearing only the area between your rods and the baited area, leaving as much weed as is practical in the baited area itself. This should afford enough cover to give fish the confidence to feed, yet still allow space to play them in.

As far as I am concerned, weed-raking is a last resort, and I far prefer to place my baits in natural clear spots within attractive weedy areas. By casting around and dragging the lead over the lake bed these are usually quite easy to locate, and are a bonus, as they allow far superior bait and rig presentation. Providing your tackle is up to the job, and the weed isn't too dense, it shouldn't be too difficult to haul fish out.

Different swims have different characteristics which will dictate how I set about baiting them; this applies to loose-feeding particles, cereal groundbaiting, boilies or

Simon getting some more bait out to keep the tench feeding

Lucky NUMBERS

TV GAME 05

HOW TO PLAY

On Friday 28th June at 7pm you should tune into ITV and watch Lucky Numbers. There is £20,000 to be won if you play our home viewer game.

On your card you will see three lucky number grids. Each grid contains 15 numbers. During the Lucky Numbers show if a number is highlighted on the show and appears on any one of your three grids then you can cross it off. If by the end of the home game in the show, you have crossed off all 15 numbers on any one grid you can claim a share of £20,000. Remember to win, you must cross off all 15 numbers on either the top, middle or bottom grid.

TREBLE CHANCE

HOW TO CLAIM

Claim your TV prize by phoning our hotline on 0191 564 0908 between 7.30pm - 9.30pm on Friday 28th June or on Saturday 29th June between 9am and noon. You must have your card with you when you phone. No claims will be accepted outside these hours. In the event of more than one valid claim, the prize will be shared equally among the winners. In the event of no valid claim the prize will be added to next week's TV prize.

Winners **MUST** agree to the publication of their names and photographs in the announcement of the results in The Sun and the filmed presentation to prize winners if applicable.

To check the numbers which appeared during the show ring the following number

0891 405005

Calls cost (per minute) 39p cheap rate, 49p other times.

NEXT WEEK'S LUCKY NUMBERS AND LAS VEGAS SUPER KENO CARD WILL BE FREE INSIDE THE SUN ON FRIDAY 5th JULY

Lucky Numbers created by Terry Mardell Organisation Ltd.

28th June. CHANCE ONE   00283   12223

| 6 | 16 | 18 | 19 | 21 |
| 37 | 38 | 40 | 42 | 44 |

28th June. CHANCE TWO   00284   12224

| 2 | 5 | 6 | 10 | 18 |
| 35 | 36 | 39 | 40 | 45 |

28th June. CHANCE THREE   00285   12225

4	5	7	8	13
20	21	26	30	31
23	24	25	29	32
36	38	39	43	45

THE SUN LAS VEGAS £1,000,000 KENO

TO BE WON EVERY DAY **UP TO £1,000,000**

THE SUN LAS VEGAS SUPER KENO

The Sun is giving you a chance to win £1,000,000 every day with Las Vegas Super Keno. Every day the Super Keno numbers are drawn live from The Flamingo Hilton, Las Vegas and published in The Sun. All you have to do is check the numbers published in The Sun against the 20 unique numbers on your card for that day. If you have marked off 13 numbers or more on any card you've won. Check the prize pay-out grid to see how much money you have won.

HOW TO CLAIM

Claim your prize for The Sun Las Vegas Super Keno game by phoning our hotline on 0171 481 3388 (0044 171 for readers in the Irish Republic) the same day between 9.30am and 3pm. You must have your card with you when you phone. No claims will be accepted outside these hours. Cards are freely available from News International Offices. For Las Vegas Super Keno numbers call 0171 782 7173

NUMBERS MATCHED	PRIZE VALUE
20	£1,000,000
19	£1,000,000
18	£1,000,000
17	£1,000,000
16	£1,000,000
15	£50,000
14	£5,000
13	£50

Friday 28 June   20565   44446

| 03 | 14 | 16 | 24 | 27 | 33 | 37 | 41 | 45 |
| 51 | 54 | 56 | 58 | 59 | 62 | 64 | 70 | 73 | 77 |

Saturday 29 June   20567   44447

| 04 | 06 | 09 | 12 | 13 | 14 | 18 | 24 | 35 | 37 |
| 41 | 45 | 46 | 48 | 52 | 53 | 58 | 66 | 68 | 77 |

Monday 1 July   20568   44448

| 05 | 15 | 24 | 33 | 37 | 40 | 41 | 44 | 45 | 47 |
| 52 | 55 | 56 | 58 | 60 | 65 | 68 | 71 | 74 | 80 |

Tuesday 2 July   20569   44449

| 13 | 14 | 18 | 20 | 21 | 22 | 24 | 26 | 27 | 38 |
| 41 | 43 | 44 | 47 | 53 | 54 | 56 | 66 | 67 | 69 |

Wednesday 3 July   20570   44450

| 14 | 15 | 27 | 29 | 30 | 38 | 39 | 43 | 47 | 50 |
| 55 | 57 | 59 | 60 | 62 | 64 | 65 | 66 | 69 | 69 |

Thursday 4 July   44450

| 01 | 09 | 11 | 12 | 15 | 19 | 20 | 31 | 35 | 38 |
| 45 | 46 | 50 | 51 | 52 | 59 | 62 | 64 | 71 | 78 |

THE Sun
Flamingo
HILTON
LAS VEGAS
LAS VEGAS
super
Keno®
UP TO
£1,000,000
TO BE WON EVERY DAY

THE Sun
Play
ITV
Lucky
NUMBERS
YOUR
£20,000
GAME EVERY FRIDAY

any other baits. Tight baiting in a single area can be effective, especially during short sessions. However, generally I prefer to spread the bait out a little over a well defined area, rather than getting the fish feeding shoulder to shoulder in one spot as I feel this increases the chance of picking up a few fish without spooking the others.

Which approach we use for baiting up deserves careful consideration, simply because fish behaviour can be so full of anomalies. When the fish are tightly grouped, for example when they are on the spawning grounds, baiting is unlikely to be a challenging issue – provided they are feeding, all that is required to keep the bobbins flying is to introduce a few baits after each bite. This is tench fishing at its easiest. The fish are there for a reason and no amount of angling pressure is likely to move them until they are ready to go. Other than getting the rigs sorted out, all we need do is trickle in a little bait in order to draw the fish down to feed.

Outside this scenario baiting can be much more complicated. Deep waters especially seem to be far more difficult to bait successfully, mostly because locating the fish can be such a hit-or-miss affair. The greater the number of features present, the more complex the whole issue becomes. If you bait just one of these features you could be lucky and come up trumps – but these long shots are not often successful.

This is where it can pay dividends to 'be methodical'. Most anglers when confronted with this situation choose to bait the most pronounced gravel bar in front of them, probably in the belief that tench are lovers of shallow water, apparently substantiated when they are seen rolling over shallow bars. In fact the tench are probably swimming around in mid-water and only breaking surface when they swim over the top of the weed growing above the bar.

While they may stop and feed on the bar, they are just as likely to drop down and feed in deep water many yards behind it. So rather than baiting just one of these options, it is preferable to cover both at the same time. Use the feed to explore the different possibilites by baiting two or three interesting areas at various depths, or perhaps lay the bait in a line which covers both the shallower feature and the deeper trough alongside.

One friend of mine used this approach on a particularly difficult water – he laid a long line of boilies from the margin to a point 60 yards out, then positioned the hookbaits at three points along this line of bait, one at each end and one in the middle. Perhaps this was being methodical in the extreme, but it certainly got results!

It would be quite possible to discuss baiting approaches for many pages. However, a picture can say a thousand words, so Diagram 34, Figs A and B, illustrate two possible baiting scenarios which would resolve some of the guesswork in baiting. They work by covering more patrolling fish, and take into account the possibility that different parts of a swim can be productive at different times of the day.

There are other ways of achieving this: for example, by baiting two or three totally different but equally attractive areas of a swim, so covering three distinct possibilities (Diagram 35, Figs A and B). Many anglers may find this all too much hassle, and fish can certainly be caught without adopting complex approaches. However,

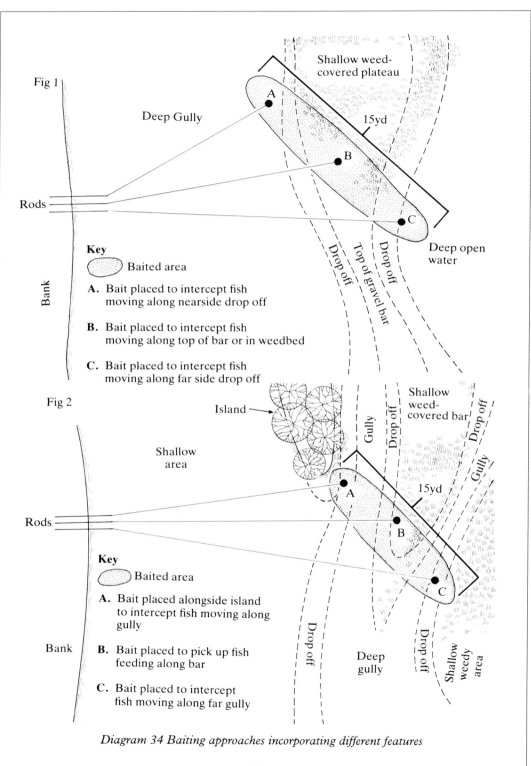

Diagram 34 Baiting approaches incorporating different features

Fig 1

Shallow weed-covered plateau

Deep Gully

A

15yd

B

Rods

C

Deep open water

Drop off
Top of gravel bar
Drop off
Drop off

Key

Baited area

A. Bait placed to intercept fish moving along nearside drop off

B. Bait placed to intercept fish moving along top of bar or in weedbed

C. Bait placed to intercept fish moving along far side drop off

Bank

Fig 2

Island

Shallow area

Gully

Drop off

Shallow weed-covered bar

Drop off

Gully

A

15yd

Rods

B

C

Key

Baited area

A. Bait placed alongside island to intercept fish moving along gully

B. Bait placed to pick up fish feeding along bar

C. Bait placed to intercept fish moving along far gully

Bank

Drop off

Deep gully

Drop off

Shallow weedy area

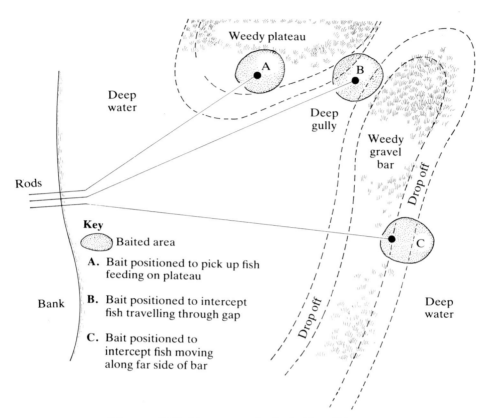

Weedy plateau

Deep
water

A

B

Deep
gully

Weedy
gravel
bar

Drop off

Rods

Key

Baited area

A. Bait positioned to pick up fish
feeding on plateau

Bank

B. Bait positioned to intercept
fish travelling through gap

Drop off

Deep
water

C. Bait positioned to
intercept fish moving
along far side of bar

C

Diagram 35 Baiting approaches by baiting different areas

how often do you see an angler struggle, often for days at a time; and when he
vacates the swim, another moves in, baits a different area and has a red letter day?
Had the first chap been more experimental, he may well have made some headway.

How much bait do we need to use? Tench can eat their way through a considerable amount of bait, and sometimes it seems that the more bait you pile in, the better
your returns will be. Nevertheless there is a limit, beyond which too much feed will
backfire; it will either feed the fish off the hookbaits, or if carp are present, draw
them onto the bait – and nothing can be more effectively guaranteed to push the
tench out.

Otherwise there is always the chance of picking up fish on single baits accompanied by only a few freebies, or perhaps a few boilies on a stringer. This is an
exploratory approach and not one I would rely on for the majority of my fishing, but
when all your best laid plans start collapsing and you are left scratching for bites, it
is surprising how often it can search out a fish or two.

We are told that the fundamental principle on which to base our baiting is to offer a steady stream of feed to attract and pin down a number of fish, while at the same time keeping them competing with each other, so that their greed overcomes caution of the hookbaits. This is fine in theory, but in practice it can be very difficult to achieve with big fish. Most of the time, we will be lucky if we can negotiate a balance between feeding them off the hookbaits, or failing to hold them in the swim, after which it could be a long wait for their return. Remember we are not talking about large numbers of hungry shoalies here, but small groups of big, well fed fish – a very different proposition. While occasionally nothing goes wrong, very often we are struggling for bites; when all we can do, apart from moving, is fish for one bite at a time and worry about the next later.

On more difficult big fish waters such as Queenford and Wilstone, most anglers adopt a 24-hour baiting procedure which is usually conducted from a dinghy. Often they will be fishing excessive distances, which makes regular and accurate feeding impossible; and with bites likely to be the exception rather than the rule, this procedure may be the only sensible approach to take.

On more prolific venues there is always the risk of fish mopping up all the feed, and then moving on before you can top the swim up. Therefore wherever practical, I prefer a more steady 'little and often' approach. How little and how often is dependent on how regularly these bites come. Inevitably this sounds vague; sometimes tench can clean up an awful lot of feed and still be catchable, on other occasions just the odd pouch now and then seems more effective. My experience is that it pays to err on the light side: it's easy enough to top a swim up, but impossible to take it out once you've piled too much in. However, circumstances do vary so much on each water, the best policy is really to take each as you find it. Be prepared to experiment, but avoid being too hasty with your conclusions.

Accuracy in baiting and casting is essential, though at longer distances this can be very tricky indeed. 'Close to' just isn't good enough: it needs to land spot on time after time. However, light values change throughout the day, altering our perception of distance over water, and playing subtle tricks with our judgement. At 70 yards, even baited areas 30 feet wide can get lost and our casts end off-target, without our knowing it.

The most popular way of overcoming this problem is to identify the reflection of an object on the opposite bank to use as a target. In still conditions this works well enough, but as soon as a good ripple comes up it becomes very difficult, and in a real blow quite impossible. During short sessions I often use this method, combined with a good measure of guesswork. It is the distance away, rather than the width of the baited area which tends to confuse our judgement. One useful trick is to mark the line with Tipp-Ex at the correct distance, so the cast can be stopped as the line comes off the spool. Or the plumbing rig can be left out throughout the session to act as a target – although this is not entirely satisfactory as it provides one more unnecessary tight line across the swim in which to get fouled up and scare fish.

Over long sessions proper markers are invaluable: Diagram 36 shows a number of different ones which can be constructed. Fig 1 comes into its own in deeper water, though is not limited to that use. However, it can only be positioned from a dinghy. Pinpoint the feature to be baited, which I usually do with a sonar fish-finder, then lower the marker – which is pre-constructed on a spool of line – into place until the lead hits bottom. The stop-knot is then slid to exactly the right depth so that the float cocks perfectly, and the line above it is snipped with a pair of scissors.

Fig 2 shows an adaption of this marker which I developed to be cast from the bank when a dinghy cannot be used. This rig is set up exactly as the last one, only

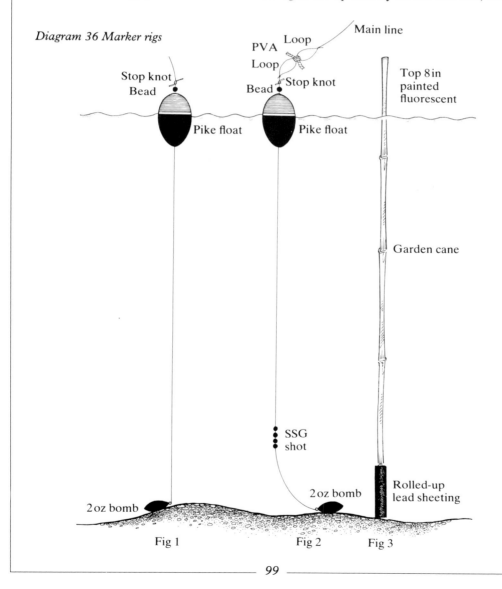

Diagram 36 Marker rigs

An 8lb 14oz which fell to a stringer cast far out in 17 feet of water

this time on a rod and line. It will then have to be cast repeatedly, adjusting the stop-knot each time until the depth has been set. After this, cut the line above the stop-knot and tie two loops, one above the stop-knot and one on the end of the main line. The two loops are then tied firmly together with plenty of PVA string.

Unfortunately this set-up is difficult to use when casting into deep water, unless used in conjunction with a rod with rings large enough to allow free passage of the PVA knot. By casting the marker a little beyond the intended area, it can be guided back into the exact position. Then enough line is reeled in to submerge the float until the PVA dissolves and the float pops back up. Usually you will find that at this point the float tends to lie on its side. To prevent this, I pinch a few swanshot on the line a little above the lead which will cock it and greatly aid visibility.

One of the problems with these markers is that hooked fish occasionally get behind them during the fight and drag them out of position; inevitably they drop down into deeper water, never to be seen again. However, in shallower areas the marker shown in Fig 3 will pull over and allow the line to pass over it without getting dragged off course; it then pops back to the surface. Once again, this marker can only be set in place from a dinghy.

A very happy Barry Snape with his punt-caught 9lb 14oz fish from a Cheshire mere

7

TENCH AND THE SWIMFEEDER

Stephen Harper

Like most young anglers in the late 1960s, I began my tench fishing in the mighty shadows of Walker and the Taylor brothers. Tench-fishing in those days had changed very little since the war and revolved around float fishing (always with a quill) and light legering methods and tench, to me, seemed comparatively hard to catch. One tench was a memorable day: two was exceptional, and any more than that in a session was a 'red letter'day. When I first fished Wolterton Park Lake (or the Marsh as it later became known) in the early 1970s, it was therefore the quill and the light leger that formed the mainstay in tactics.

Wolterton is probably one of the most beautiful lakes I have had the privilege to fish. Nestling in the heart of north Norfolk, amongst secluded parkland, it has an atmosphere all its own. The approach is down the long gravel drive, through the tennis courts, then beneath a canopy formed by extensive and colourful rhododendron bushes and finally out onto the meadows that surround the lake.

An impressive mansion, the seat of Lord Walpole, overlooks the lake from the higher ground, whilst the meadows slope gently down to it, studded with oak and beech. Grassland surrounding the lake is cropped close by cattle and even deer and forms almost a lawn, heavily soiled by the debris of many Canada geese, swans and a multitude of other water fowl, some apparently quite rare.

The lake itself is around 8–10 acres in extent; an ancient boathouse and a small island of tangled trees and deadwood add to its character. A small inlet flows into the shallows, whilst at the other end the water flows out via an outlet on the dam. Here the water is at its deepest, extending to a central channel along much of the lake, although depths rarely exceed 4ft. The shallow margins extend out into the lake for several yards all around and the bottom is heavily silted. At certain times, daphnia clouds the clear water and bloodworm fills the silt, providing a ready-made larder for the tench.

(top) *The sun sets over the point swim at Johnsons*
(below left) *Chris Burt was so overjoyed with this 9lb 1oz fish that he bought a pint for the horse in the field behind his swim;* (below right) *Unfortunately on this occasion it was the bream which weighed doubles at 11lb 7oz. The tench came in at 8lb 1oz*

TENCH AND THE SWIMFEEDER

The usual approach in the early days at the lake was to bait a small area with a groundbait mixture and to fish a dark bait, such as lobworm, over it so the bait would contrast and stand out well. Another rod would be baited with a light-coloured bait, such as breadflake or maggot (or a cocktail of both) and fished just on the edge of the groundbaited area, hopefully standing out against the dark lake bed.

These tactics worked, and we even had the odd 'red letter' day – but as for setting the angling world alight, there was little chance of that! And yet the lake was full of tench. At spawning time in early summer they could be seen clearly in their hundreds on the shallows, from the smallest of around a pound, to the big, pot-bellied females: but why couldn't they be caught in any numbers? It soon became obvious that our tactics were not efficient or refined enough to trick these wary fish in such gin-clear water. The lake was crammed with natural food and the tench simply didn't want our offerings badly enough to risk capture. One or two were always fooled, but not consistently nor in any great numbers.

It also became apparent later that the larger baits used in traditional tench fishing, such as lobworms and flake, would never fully preoccupy these tench and make their capture easy.

Before the 1970s the lake had been choked with weed, the only clear patches being those made by anglers who were restricted to float fishing and legering close in. Then in the new decade came a drastic change: the weed simply disappeared. It is possible that spraying by the landowner to kill weeds and thistles around the lake was responsible. Seepage into the lake obviously occurred and as the seasons passed the other species such as rudd, perch and pike, all gradually died off leaving only the hardy tench to proliferate.

For now the lake had changed dramatically: apart from the odd patch of stubborn weed here and there, it was barren; beneath the surface of the water a stark desert replaced the previous forest of weed. This opened up the lake to a new method of angling, however, a method that would revolutionise the fishing there and write a chapter in the history and development of modern tench fishing – the swimfeeder.

No part of the lake was now safe for the tench population, not even the very centre where for years they had been free from the attentions of anglers. With the new method came fast taper rods, pre-stretched lines, and small but strong forged hooks to withstand the heavy pressure of solid striking at distance against heavy fish.

The local anglers that first used the swimfeeder at Wolterton were obviously not the first to recognise the potential of this simple leaded tube of plastic. In particular, Bob Church of Northampton had already had considerable success in deep lakes in the Midlands and had written an article in the June 1971 issue of *Angling* magazine to this effect. It was this article and his success that prompted me to try the swimfeeder at Wolterton, but what a dismal failure that first attempt turned out to be. Instead of open-ended feeders, I used block-end; I mixed the groundbait far too wet, and on the retrieve it remained in the feeder: a total disaster, and at the time I failed to see how anyone could achieve success with a contraption that made such a commotion as it entered the water.

A little perseverance and fine tuning was called for, and I believe it was John Judge who finally pointed us all in the right direction. The secret was to fish open-ended feeders packed with almost dry groundbait at either end and maggots in the centre. On impact with the water, the contents literally exploded out and gradually settled all around the hookbait.

That first season of the swimfeeder at Wolterton, in the summer of 1975, proved to be phenomenal for the local anglers lucky enough to be involved. Once the method has been mastered to some degree and the initial problems ironed out – rods too sloppy, lines too stretchy, hooks too weak – tench began to fill the landing nets like never before at Wolterton. Three, four, five in a session became the norm rather than the exception, and even bags of a dozen fish were not unheard of.

That first season passed by with the general size of fish ranging from around 4lb to nearly 6lb, but nothing over that weight. Still, in those days a five-pounder was the 'target weight', though a six-pounder, the dream-weight then, was to follow once we were convinced this was feasible.

Sure enough, on the opening morning of the next season, Martyn Page, John Wilson and I all caught six-pounders (Martyn's the largest at 6lb 6oz) along with an

Martyn Page, Steve Harper and John Wilson pose with Wolterton Park's first 6s

incredible bag of tench, the majority of them well over 5lb. It seemed we had 'cracked' the water with the help of the swimfeeder, an almost weed-free lake, and a tiny bait (maggots) that could preoccupy the tench in areas of the lake where they were not used to being hooked.

For the rest of that summer until late August when bites became fewer, we fished the lake along with several other local anglers, each of whom bettered their personal best tench time and time again. Along the way, we refined the method and added to its effectiveness. We tried other baits besides maggots in the feeder, chopped lob-worms or brandlings being particularly successful – but still nothing as effective as the humble maggot. Tucking the hookbait into the feeder as it was loaded also proved a useful dodge; this avoided tangles during the cast, and in later seasons when we began to use long confidence hooklinks, it ensured that the hookbait always lay close to the feeder (as long as the groundbait mixture was correct).

The tench obviously became attuned to the sound of the feeders hitting the water, recognising this as a sign of imminent food. The bobbins would often be wrenched from our hands as they were being set immediately after casting, and John Judge even had a rod dragged into the lake on one occasion by an over-zealous tench, just managing to grab the butt before it disappeared!

I fished the lake as often as I could during this season, usually in the company of Martyn Page. We even made the effort to fish a few hours before work on several days during each week, the long journey made worth while for even a short period when such wonderful sport was guaranteed.

As the summer became cooler and days shorter, bites gradually became fewer; so we moved onto carp and zander and wondered what the next season would bring at Wolterton Park Lake.

By now, news had inevitably leaked out onto the big-fish grapevine that large tench, and many of them, were being caught from a Norfolk lake. Some well known and highly successful anglers travelled to Norfolk for the following season and it didn't take the more skilful long to realise that the open-ended swimfeeder, com-bined with maggots, was 'the' method.

The season began quietly for Wolterton, the weather conditions not helping mat-ters; rain and gale force winds prevailed and very low air and water temperatures for that time of year. In spite of more anglers around the lake, the tench were playing hard to get; in fact, it seemed that they had 'wised up' somewhat to our method. It was usual to fish three or four maggots on a size 12 hook to a 5lb feeder-link, but it was not until we began to scale down that bites again became more frequent. Two and even one maggot on a size 16 or 14 hook to 4lb or 3lb feeder-links began once again to bring results.

A few days into the season and the tench began to appear again regularly and one thing became crystal clear – they had grown! Four-pounders were rare, five-pounders common, six-pounders the norm and, for the first time, came the sevens; truly mind-blowing fish for 1977. Kevin Clifford was the first to catch a seven at the

Steve Harper returning two chunky 6s to the Marsh

lake, at 7lb 6oz; it was a new Norfolk and lake record, but it lasted only a short period because I was lucky to follow Kevin's fish with a 7lb 4oz tench, and shortly after another seven at 7lb 10½ oz. Not a huge tench now, but the Norfolk record still stands at 'only' 8lb 2oz today (1991).

Other sevens followed that year – not many, but Martyn did take three to 7lb 5oz in 24 hours, possibly the first angler ever to do so.

The 1977 season had proved hard in comparison to the first seasons at Wolterton with the swimfeeder. The tench were fewer but larger, but also it seemed they were becoming very wary of maggots. And then towards the tail-end of the summer the weed began to make an unwelcome return, much of it floating and causing many problems with bite detection. For 1978 it seemed we would have to revise our tactics if we were to keep one step ahead of the tench, and the weed.

The new season dawned and once again saw a deterioration in sport. Within a few weeks the weed was a major problem, and casting around for clear patches and raking narrow strips far into the lake became the usual procedure. The tench did come out, still to maggots and swimfeeder, but from the heady days of the earlier seasons when we had first used the swimfeeder it was now very hard work indeed.

Initially the tench had been attracted to the splash of the feeders, recognising this as a signal of free food. Now, however, it was obviously registering danger, and long waits in between casts became usual. Runs came out of the blue when you were least expecting them, sometimes around midday when the summer sun was at its height. However, when they came, they were often well worth waiting for. Kevin Clifford managed several 'sevens' that season to around 7½ lb, a weight that remained the ceiling weight for Wolterton tench over the years, although the odd fish did exceed it by a few ounces.

During the following seasons, the introduction of sweetcorn instead of maggots with the swimfeeder brought about a brief revival of fortunes at the lake. Some good bags of fish were once again recorded, proving that maggot was regarded as dangerous by the tench.

Unfortunately, as the eighties dawned, the weed returned to such an extent that the use of the swimfeeder became nonsensical. It is highly probable that many hook-baits never reached the bottom, but were hung up in the weed and therefore almost totally ineffective.

The catch rate dwindled to an all-time low. Apart from a very few hardcore regulars, anglers deserted the lake as it became increasingly difficult. Many factors probably contributed to this, the main one being the return of the weed which made feeder fishing very difficult; and any tench that did eventually pick up a bait had a very good chance of slipping the hook in the weed. The weed also brought with it an abundance of natural food, and altogether the tench seemed much less in evidence – they were old fish, and a few hard winters plus the heavy angling pressure must have taken their toll. To cap it all, those few that remained seemed to have wised up to maggot and corn and swimfeeders and those tell-tale patches of groundbait that lay here and there about the lake bed. I did in fact develop a swimfeeder that alleviated this problem: called a 'spring dropper', it would deliver maggots, corn, hemp, worms, or any other baits into the swim but without the use of the groundbait. Unfortunately the dense weed now caused problems for any type of feeder and it never reached its true potential at the lake.

Eventually, towards the end of the 1980s, Wolterton, once so prolific, became a byword for the most difficult of waters. Several days fishing around the clock would yield not one sign of a tench – the last decent fish to come from the lake, a 7lb 12oz specimen, fell to the rod of Dave Humphries in 1988, probably the last angler to throw in the towel at Wolterton.

Another Marsh fish comes to Steve's net

Tench fishing at the lake has now turned full circle. From the 1960s, with traditional methods; and through the seventies, with the arrival of the swimfeeder, for a few short seasons the lake came to the forefront of the big fish angling world because of a set of circumstances that occurred together: a lack of weed, the swimfeeder, and anglers determined to reap the rewards of an astonishingly successful method – in a lake ideally suited to it if only briefly.

With the return of the weed and a dwindling, educated tench population the lake once again became very hard, and the circle was complete when, finally, life became too short to tench-fish at Wolterton Park Lake at all.

Today, angling at the lake is not allowed. With the death of Lord Walpole and the succession of his son, the fishing has been stopped, so who knows what the future holds for the lake? One thing is certain though; a water such as Wolterton thrives on neglect, and I like to think that one day I shall fish there again with that grand house as a backdrop, and watch the deer beneath the beech trees, and wait for those bobbins to move once again.

8

THE EVOLUTION OF TC TENCHING

Tony Miles

The way in which my tench fishing methods evolved during my eight-year association with TC pit in Oxfordshire is one of the most fascinating aspects of my long career in pursuit of big fish. Trefor West and I first fished TC on opening day 1977, and it is important to realise the background to that first visit. We had known of the pit for a few years, and also knew that it contained good tench and bream; but neither of us realised quite how big the tench grew, until a friend of ours caught a specimen of 7lb 14oz, a truly colossal fish for those days. That was in the summer of 1976, and Trefor and I decided to give the water some serious attention from the following June.

Initially, our information was that the water contained very few fish, but of a large average size. The consensus of opinion among the few anglers who fished it was that it was fatal to use much cereal feed; in fact the universal approach was the use of the swimfeeder in conjunction with a long tail of light line to a 16 or 18 hook, baited with one or two maggots, at long range. The few fish caught had succumbed to this method and, not unnaturally, it was assumed that this method was the one most likely to succeed. Bites, we were told, were extremely finicky.

Trefor and I went to the water in June 1977 with very open minds, giving full respect to the other anglers' opinions and experiences, but quite intent on adapting our approach to our observations. As early as the second day of our first trip, we had realised that a lot of things were simply not adding up. First of all, there were only three other anglers on the water on opening day, and when we spoke to them it transpired that three anglers on any one day was very unusual: it was normally fewer than that!

This information convinced us that the use of very light tackle and small hooks and baits was totally illogical. Firstly, how could the tench possibly be tackle-shy on a water which received such minimal angling pressure? Second, the evidence of our own eyes told us that there was a much bigger head of tench present than we had been led to believe. The amount of rolling at dawn confirmed that. Third, the long-range approach was at odds with the numbers of big tench seen patrolling the margins at dusk.

This evidence was sufficient for Trefor and me to decide to adopt a totally different approach to the fishing. We would groundbait very heavily with both cereal feed and bait samples, at close range of no more than thirty yards out, and fish over the feed with large baits on big hooks. By using a decent lead in conjunction with a fairly short tail, we felt that we should get positive bites on our big baits.

During that first summer we managed catches of three or more fish on most trips, something which had been a comparative rarity before. As well as that, a new personal best of 7lb 2oz to Trefor gave us all the extra enthusiasm we required.

That 1977 summer was really the testing ground at this new water, and it was from 16 June 1978 that our approach began to pay dividends. During the evening of the 15th I introduced into my selected swim – a clean gravel bar about thirty yards offshore – 20lb of pure breadcrumbs, plus a hundred or more flake samples, chopped lobs and half a catering can of sweetcorn. Over the next few weeks that swim was to yield me several catches of five or six tench, with most of them 5lb plus; though it was opening day itself which proved the highlight of that summer.

My baits had been cast at dawn, on a beautiful calm June morning. There was a chilly mist in the air, promising a hot day to come, and I was soon sitting comfortably amongst the rushes and the beds of yellow iris, a hot mug of tea in my hand, watching two motionless swingtips. To the left of the swim, a fluffy lump of flake lay in ambush amongst the loose feed while a lobworm was similarly positioned to the right. For about five hours tench rolled regularly over the feed, yet not a bite could I get. The sun rose higher in the sky and it became very hot. A good bite on flake was inexplicably missed at about 11am, and I decided to rebait with three grains of corn. Although not a particularly logical decision, it was to prove a decisive one.

Scarcely had I balanced the swingtip after the cast when it fell back sharply, before shooting out straight. The rod was sliding forward in the rests as I grabbed the handle and set the hook into a powerful resistance that surged irresistibly to my left. That opening day tench gave me a tussle fitting for a new personal best, for so it turned out to be. For five minutes the battle ebbed and flowed until I eventually breathed a sigh of relief as a huge fish slid into the net: 6lb 15oz it weighed, the fulfilment of a dream I had harboured for many years. At last I had caught a 6lb tench.

Because of the limited attention from other anglers, we were able to keep our methods and catches to ourselves for the rest of the 1978 summer, and throughout the following season as well. By the end of the 1979 summer our big bait, heavy feed technique was regularly producing catches of eight to a dozen good fish whereas the other few anglers were still taking only the odd solitary tench on long-range feeder tactics. However, we knew it was only a matter of time before we were found out – though we had often said that one day we would be in the right swim at the right time and take a big bag of tench that would expose that particular water's potential far and wide. That was to come true in opening week 1980, in fact, although I did break some ground earlier than that.

In July 1979 I arrived for a three-day session, and observed many big tench rolling about forty yards out in a weedy corner of the pit. After humping a mountain of gear round the lake, I spent fifteen minutes or so watching the activity through my binoculars – I was able to observe some colossal fish, so my anticipation was at fever pitch as I assembled my temporary home.

As most of the activity was too far from the bank for the swim to be fed by hand, I spent some considerable time catapulting about forty small balls of groundbait to the area. I had also brought with me a gallon of maggots with the intention of trying the feeder on one rod, but casting very regularly and using it in conjunction with a hookbait of maggot and flake cocktail. Because of the range, the feeder would allow me to present a bait among free feed, and this would be further enhanced by cupping groundbait around the base of the feeder on each cast. Before starting to fish, I also prepared another swim just over the marginal rushes to my left and baited it heavily. I intended to float fish the margins at dusk, an approach that had been very much neglected at TC.

By midday, I had two feeder rods in position on the longer range swim, and the first two bites were not long in coming, two 5lb tench being brought to net in quick succession. Both were males and gave me exhilarating battles in the shallow weedy water. Then at about mid-afternoon I started to experience infuriating little tweaks and lifts of the tip, which led to two or three abortive strikes. I wondered whether small fish were twitching at the ends of the maggots, so after another fruitless strike, I rebaited with flake only, using a much larger piece on a bigger hook – I had been using a size 10 but had now reverted to a 6.

About ten minutes after I had recast, the swingtip shot to the horizontal without any preliminaries, and as I struck there was a tremendous vortex over the swim as a big fish rolled. I knew I had hooked a giant of a tench. Like most tench, this one gave a tremendous account of itself and it was several minutes before I was on my knees, admiring a fish that appeared simply colossal – even when the scales had settled on 7lb 12oz I hardly believed it was true. And I experienced another 'first' that evening when I took three nice fish to 5lb 14oz in half-an-hour at dusk, on laid-on lobs in the marginal swim. At long last I really felt that things were starting to come together.

In hindsight, it was the capture of my 7lb 12oz fish which led to Trefor and I rapidly losing our peace and quiet at TC, although it was inevitable eventually. During the close season of 1980 I was persuaded to contribute an article on tench fishing to our local paper, and I rather naively illustrated it with a superb colour slide of my big fish. In his wisdom, the editor used it in large format on the front cover, and as the paper was circulated throughout the Midlands, the size of the tench acted as a magnet for big fish men. When Trefor and I arrived at the start of the 1980 season, the water was packed.

Despite this, the swim where I had taken my seven-pounder was vacant, and so we moved in for a week's very intense fishing. We had decided on further refinements to our technique: not only would we step up the groundbaiting, we would also rake the swims regularly and ensure that the groundbait was introduced with absolute accuracy. This would be achieved by the simple expedient of Trefor swimming out to the swims towing a baby-bath full of bait whilst I directed him from the shore. Dragging was carried out in the same way.

Fishing began at first light on opening day, and Trefor and I made a tremendous catch of big tench over the next seven days. There was only one fish from over thirty which was under 5lb, and we had several six- and seven-pounders, topped off by another personal best of 7lb 13oz to Trefor. It was impossible to keep such a catch of fish quiet, and after that week our secret was well and truly out. Heavy accurate baiting and using large hookbaits became the standard approach, resulting in numbers of tench being caught that would have been thought impossible a few short years previously.

The predictable result of the much heavier angling pressure was that the tench soon began to wise up to the technique we were applying and bites became more finicky. I managed to overcome this problem, however, by fishing much shorter hooklinks in conjunction with heavy leads – bolt rigs, obviously – and therefore still experienced galloping runs when other anglers were exasperated by twitchers.

Dave Boulstridge with a humpbacked beauty weighing 8lb 12oz

Eventually, however, this tactic too became less effective, and I had to revert to the swimfeeder with two or three maggots to keep catching consistently. Even with the feeder, though, I utilised very short tails with heavy fixed feeders and so I had belting runs off the fish; and this approach led to the capture of my biggest-ever TC tench, on a day that was memorable in more ways than one.

In September 1980 on a mild and drizzly morning Trefor and I arrived for a further two days at TC. Trefor had decided to have a crack for one of the water's huge bream, but I was intent on my search for an 8lb tench. Earlier that season a friend of ours, Dave Boulstridge, had taken a fish of 8lb 12oz on his first visit to the water, and that had really put an edge on my big tench appetite.

Trefor set up his stall off the main road bank, the favoured area for bream at the time, while I assessed likely areas a long way to his right, in the shallows. Several rolls from good fish, about 50 yards out from the weedy corner of the pit decided me to establish my base there. It was the first time I had ever fished the swim. The main problem was the volume of weed, and I spent some time casting around with a sliding float and heavy lead looking for a weed-free feature of some kind. I soon located a very shallow, but clean gravel bar, about 1 1/2 feet deep, running about 20 yards left to right.

I decided to place one bait at each side of this feature, and then made about ten casts to each area with a feeder full of maggots to establish a bed of bait; with two baits in position, I settled down to wait. The terminal rig on each rod was the same – a loaded feeder, with a swanshot pinched 2in above it to make it into a shock rig. A short tail of 6in was completed by a size 12 hook baited with two maggots on one rod and a maggot and flake cocktail on the other.

For about two hours the bobbins remained motionless and I reclined contentedly, enjoying the peace and quiet of that damp autumn day. The bite, when it came, was sudden and vicious. Without warning, the bobbin on the maggot rod rocketed to the butt and the reel began backwinding furiously. As I set the hook, a huge fish thrashed at the surface a long way out, heralding the start of a memorable battle. The volume of weed meant that the outcome would not be certain until the folds of the net safely enveloped the fish, and so I played that tench with all the skill and experience at my command. Once I had brought it over the worst of the weed I could breathe a little easier, but it was still several minutes before I could take a good look at my antagonist as it fought deep and stubbornly in the marginal channel. Eventually the unrelenting pressure told, and a magnificient tench was drawn over the waiting net.

Apart from the fact that it was bloody big and it had two very distinctive parallel scars on the flank, close to the dorsal, should it ever be recaptured, that tench would be unmistakeable. The scales revealed 7lb 13oz, but even though I had convinced myself the fish would go over 8lb, it was impossible to be disappointed. What a superb tench, a new personal best by one ounce. After the fish had been witnessed and photographed by Trefor, it was slipped back, and swam away strongly.

That tench was the only one I had from that shallow bar, and about four hours after I decided to wind in the flake rod and fish a big bait into 4 feet or so of water next to some marginal rushes to my right, only about 2 yards out. Having changed the terminal rig to a heavy fixed lead, I baited a size 6 hook with the biggest lobworm I could find and swung it out. I then retired back under my umbrella and put the kettle on.

The water was nowhere near boiling when the bobbin on the close-range rod shot up and the rod top lurched round. The tench I had hooked again fought very hard, not making long runs but resisting in a series of short, surging plunges, staying deep all the time. With the fish virtually under the rod top, I could hardly fail to get the best of the fight – and as it slid over the rim of the net, I saw those unmistakeable parallel scars. The mouth revealed the previous hook mark, and the fish still weighed 7lb 13oz! On two different methods, and only a few hours apart, I had taken the same personal-best fish twice in a day: that must be unique.

Tony Miles proudly displays this 7lb 13oz, his best from TC which he caught twice in one

THE EVOLUTION OF TC TENCHING

In the two years that followed I became more and more involved with the water's bream, but anyway the pattern of the tench fishing had begun to change. TC was now fished very heavily indeed, almost all the anglers fishing the feeder, and the tench were much more circumspect in their feeding; catches tailed off and many smaller fish were turning up, and by 1982 it was quite common to have several tench blanks running. However, on one memorable day an experiment with bait flavouring produced remarkable results.

I had fished for two days without success, and on the final morning decided to fish two identical feeder tackles side by side, with the maggots on one of them flavoured with pineapple. I was fishing close to Andy Barker and John Cadd that day, who had also been biteless, and we were all amazed when the flavoured baits produced a string of big tench in about two hours. During that time, the natural maggots remained untouched.

Following that first catch to flavoured maggots, several others followed, not just on pineapple but on other flavours as well, in particular vanilla and maple cream. For a short while the tench were quite taken in by this new approach, several multiple bags of fish being taken quickly; but it, too, soon lost its effectiveness.

In the 1983 season I decided to revert to big baits for my tenching, and experimented with flavoured paste baits fished in large pieces on big hooks. I started off with the flavours that had been most successful on maggots, and all the pastes I tried caught fish; undoubtedly the most successful was heavily laced with almond flavouring and coloured yellow and I will always remember the first time I ever used that bait.

Three of us were fishing adjacent swims, the two anglers either side of me presenting standard feeder rigs at range. On the first day I was using one feeder with flavoured maggots, and the other rod was baited with a large lob. At about midday on the second day, still biteless, I abandoned fishing with maggots and changed to large pieces of my new almond paste. The result of this bait change was quite spectacular. Within minutes of casting out the new paste for the first time, I was playing a tench that had taken it very viciously indeed, and this 5lb male was the first of over fifty bites that came to the bait in the next thirty hours. I lost a few fish in the weed and missed some of the bites, but still landed over thirty tench. During that hectic period I had just one fish on lobs, and the anglers either side blanked on their maggots.

That incredible catch of fish is probably my most exciting memory of TC tenching, and it was followed by two more years of terrific action. The fish wised up to each new variant fairly quickly, however, and as a counter-measure I began to make my pastes slowly dissolving, following the lead given by Alan Smith of Northampton, one of the best tench anglers I know. By putting a small amount of finely ground rusk in our paste baits, we could calculate how long they would take to disintegrate, as the rusk slowly dispersed and swelled with the action of the water – the visible effect was like fizzing, as the surface layer of a ball of paste appeared to

*Alan Rawden's smile surely hides his true feelings about this
foulhooked TC monster of 9lb 7oz*

effervesce. This obviously carried the flavour, with the result that a kind of flavoured
halo was created around the bait itself, and I believe that this is why these baits were
so successful. Depending on the activity in the swim, or the effect that I was trying
to create, the pastes could be made to dissolve more or less rapidly by altering the
amount of rusk used. The fast versions were the more successful, although they were
more difficult to fish with. The problem was, that if the bait had been out for more
than an hour or so, tench milling around the terminal tackle could actually wash the
bait away from the hook. I had several tench that must have taken the bait when it
was little more than a pile of powder with a hook in the middle. Fast dissolvers
therefore required frequent recasting, but the extra trouble was certainly worth while;

they were probably the most successful tench baits I have ever used.

I also experimented with flavoured cocktails in this 1983/85 period, and another highlight in my TC tenching career occurred on a two-day July session in 1984. I was actually after bream, and had laced my loose feed with caramel flavouring; one rod was baited with a flake/caster cocktail, the flake having been soaked in a sweetened solution of concentrated caramel, and the other was baited with lobworm. Those two nights saw no fewer than sixteen tench succumb to the flavoured flake, and every bite was a real butt-ringer, in marked contrast to the little lifts and twitches that were being experienced all the while by anglers fishing the feeder.

When I finished my association with TC in 1986, it was obvious to me where the tench fishing was heading; and sure enough, in the following summer the use of boilies became regular practice. The intense fishing pressure at TC since our introduction to that peaceful and neglected fishery in 1977 had resulted in a remarkably rapid evolution of fishing tactics. In just nine short years the tench had been transformed from the naive creatures we had first met to probably the most sophisticated in the country. And I am very pleased that I was able to play a leading role in that evolution during those very exciting years.

9

TENCH FISHING FROM A PUNT

Barry Snape

I have fished the Mere for ten years now and except for the first year, have always used a punt. Although I fish on my own, to do so requires a team effort as without the help of my pal Paul Griffiths, it would be impossible to carry out all the necessary preparations. In fact in the early days we used to fish together from the punt, but after a while we both agreed that it was not very practical due to long sessions and movement in the boat; and there was always the thought of our ending up both fishing for the same fish.

The punt I use is one of the original ones to be put on the water, thirty years old and very well built. When we originally obtained permission to use it, it was out of the water and in need of some repairs. Since this work was completed and the punt put back into use, we have made various modifications and added a few fittings, all of which have made life a bit easier when on the water. The punt measures 12ft long by 3ft 6in wide; it has a fixed seat in the centre, but we have modified the end seats so they can be removed to allow a little more room when the boat is anchored in the fishing position. We also added a pair of rowlocks, as oars allow for better control when manoeuvering the boat. On the inside around the gunnels we fitted a number of blocks into which were drilled two holes: one is just large enough to take the inside of an adjustable bank-stick, if this is cut down to about 6in long; these are used for locating keep nets or tying carp sacks. The other hole is threaded to take a brass fitting which we had drilled to hold the rod-rests and which included a thumb-screw for locking in position. Originally these were used for legering, but movement in the boat was always a problem which made them unsuitable, although I still occasionally use them for float fishing.

One of the most useful items that we fitted was a pair of anchor poles, about 12ft long, attached to the sides of the punt and located diagonally opposite each other. One end of each pole is fastened to a swivel bracket and the other end locates in a 'U' bracket (Diagram 37). This means the punt can be stopped and anchored in any position, a facility which has proved invaluable in a number of ways. While actually fishing the swivel anchor poles are not used, as they are not long enough to give sufficient hold in the silt. The preferred method for this

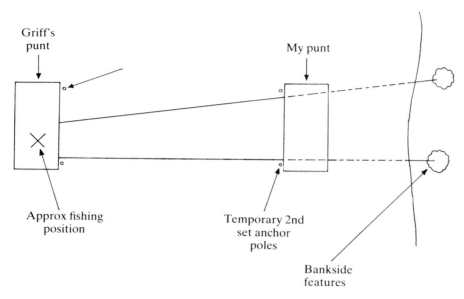

Diagram 37 Setting the swim out using two punts

is to tie the punt to scaffolding poles which we position at the neck of the swim.

Finally, a cover is one fitting which I would recommend to anyone who is thinking of building a punt or already has one; ours is purpose-built, a timber frame covered with a galvanised steel sheet which can be padlocked at each end of the punt.
Over the years other boats on the water have been vandalised: to date, ours has been
left alone. This is a real bonus, although the cover is mainly to protect the punt from
the worst of the winter weather; while we have had to carry out some minor repairs,
it has certainly reduced the cost of maintaining the boat as well as prolonging its life.

The Mere itself is 44 acres in size, roughly square in shape and typical of many
similar fisheries located in the north-west Midlands; it is shallow around the periph-
ery, gradually sloping to a maximum depth of about 7ft. There are no shelves or pronounced contours which can be identified as fish patrol routes, and the bottom is
extremely silted, to the extent that the 20ft-long scaffolding poles used to anchor the
punt can easily be pushed all the way into the silt. There is limited bankside access
to the fishery – one end is completely out of bounds, and the other three sides are
only fishable from fishing stages.

I usually start what has now become my annual tenching campaign towards the
end of April, although I also visit the Mere during the winter months to check the
punt over.

During April weed starts to proliferate as the water warms up. Eventually it trans-
forms the bottom of the Mere from its barren water moonscape into an underwater
forest, until the whole water is covered from top to bottom. The extent of its advance

and its density will inevitably influence my methods, but a weed rake is essential and usually we will be raking our respective swims a week before the start of the season. This is something to which I pay a lot of attention, as a well prepared swim can catch you fish when the going gets tough.

The aim is to rake a well defined, wedge-shaped gully, and to achieve this we employ two punts. We locate Griff's punt behind the scaffold anchor poles, which are now in a permanent position, and we start by marking out the swim, both for distance and direction. We then use my punt to position the top of the wedge. The punt's swivel poles allow us to position the boat accurately, and then a second set of scaffold poles are placed in the top corners of the wedge after being lined up with two distinctive features on the bank (Diagram 38). This will help accurate casting at night. The correct distance is set by a knot tied in the rope at about 30 yards. Originally we only used the anchor poles to hold the punt in position and marked the swim with canes, but during raking we found that the punt would be pulled out of position.

View of the mere showing the raked swim

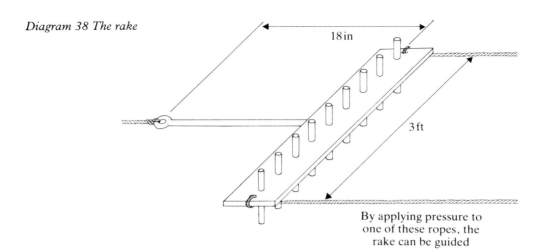

Diagram 38 The rake

18 in

3 ft

By applying pressure to one of these ropes, the rake can be guided

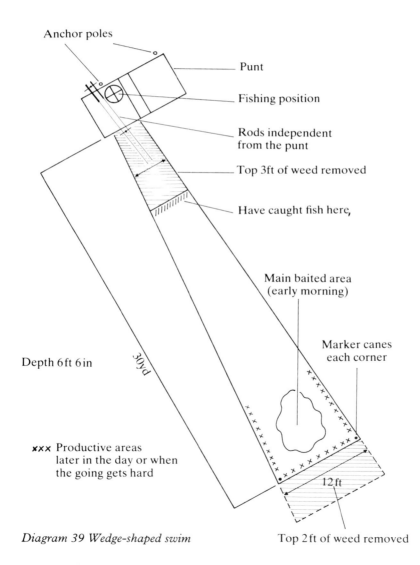

Anchor poles

Punt

Fishing position

Rods independent from the punt

Top 3ft of weed removed

Have caught fish here,

Main baited area (early morning)

Marker canes each corner

Depth 6ft 6in

30yd

xxx Productive areas later in the day or when the going gets hard

12 ft

Diagram 39 Wedge-shaped swim

Top 2ft of weed removed

Once we have set the swim out, we start the raking. The rake is especially made for the job and is attached to three ropes (Diagram 39), two of which are tied to the end of the rake and run to my boat; this allows me to guide it by applying pressure to one or other of the ropes. The third rope is fixed to the centre T-bar of the rake and runs to Griff's punt.

The rake is lowered into the swim from my position at the head of the swim and then Griff pulls it back towards his punt – although I don't rake all the way back as I like to leave some weed between my fishing position and the swim. We knot the rope from Griff's punt to allow us to rake to the same position every time, then by continually pulling the rake between the two punts an accurate wedge-shaped gully can be formed. However, depending on its density, I will sometimes leave a certain amount of weed in the centre of the swim to give the tench that little confidence. Once the raking is completed, the temporary scaffolding poles are removed and replaced with marker canes. This will allow me to cast tight to the sides of the gully.

The markers are made from garden canes painted with a sealant to help them float. At their narrow ends cords are whipped, and these are tied to anchor weights; the thicker ends are cut so that just a couple of inches protrude above the water, and these are painted fluourescent to aid casting during that extra half-hour before dawn and after dusk. Each cane acts like a giant float, allowing line to pass harmlessly over it should a hooked fish run through the back of the swim. Finally, I trim the top of the weed between the marker canes and swim and for a couple of yards behind the swim. This allows me to overcast my line without fouling the weed, so that I can fish tight up to the back of the swim.

These preparations can take a good part of the day but they are vitally important – over the years they have resulted in a good tench or two, whilst other anglers fishing the water have struggled.

Pre-baiting is an important part of my approach, and usually begins a couple of weeks before the start of the season, even before we rake. I increase the amount of bait and shorten the intervals between baiting, eventually pre-baiting once during each of the three days before the start of the season.

Once the season is underway, I anchor the boat over the swim when I am baiting before fishing so I can introduce the bait very accurately. And after finishing a session, once again I anchor the boat over the swim, this time so I can inspect the bottom with a glass-bottomed bucket. It's surprising just how much you can learn – for instance, the tench can sometimes become preoccupied with just one of the particles included in the groundbait whilst ignoring others altogether.

Briefly, my tackle comprises firstly two carbon rods, one 11ft 6in with a T.C. of 1¼lb, and one 11ft with a T.C. of 1lb; both are fitted with Mitchell 300 reels with a choice of two spools, each of 4lb and 6lb Maxima and one spool of 8lb Bayer Ultima. Hooks of size 12 and under are spade-ended, and above that size I use eyed. I also carry a large selection of floats to cater for varying weather conditions, and a selection of leger weights, together with all the other bits and pieces which make up the contents of a tackle box.

Hard at work; Barry rakes the swim from the punt

The methods I use vary, depending on the weather, weed conditions and also the reaction of the fish. My favourite technique is to float-fish using a simple lift method – partly I just like the tradition, but also there is no better sight than the float lifting a couple of inches before sliding away. So for example one day I may be fishing a lobworm fished under a Windbeater on a 6lb line with a size 10 hook, anchored with a single AA shot, and I will be expecting the bites to be bold. The next I might have a single maggot under a light float shotted down so that only ¼in of bristle is showing; bites are then indicated by a slight lifting or dipping of the float.

Obviously 4lb line is better suited both to casting and presentation. It also allows me to use whichever of my floats suits the given weather conditions, although ultimately the density of the weed will decide which line strains I choose. When the weed gets dense, 4lb line runs too great a risk of losing fish.

When fishing fine and expecting only the smallest movements of the float, I use only one rod, holding it all the time to avoid being distracted. I attach the floats with a Drennan Float Clip so I can make a quick float change if needed, to suit changes in the weather; conditions often alter during the morning. One method which has often accounted for a few fish while fishing 'light', especially when the wind is right, has been to allow the bait to drift across the swim, with the bait set a couple of feet overdepth. This is worth a try when there are fish in the swim but showing no interest in a static bait.

I can also fish the lead from the punt. I am usually on the water at around 8pm then fish through the night until around 11am the following day, and I consider legering to be the only practical method during the hours of darkness. I also prefer to leger during very windy weather. To accommodate this from the punt, I use a set of purpose-built extendable rod-rests made from conduit in 5ft-long sections which screw together. The top section is only 3ft long and has a brass fitting fixed into the top designed to take the inside section of a standard bank-stick. A locking pin allows it, if necessary, to be adjusted to 5ft long, with the top section making the rod-rests. I position one of these either side of the punt, which allows me to use Optonics successfully. Being independent of the boat, I don't have to put up with every movement of the boat being transferred to the rods. For bite indication, simple isotope bobbins are clipped onto the line, positioned to hang within the punt. This reduces false bites registering on the Optonics during windy sessions. Sometimes I use the same rod-rests for float fishing, but generally I prefer to hold the rod as this can often make the difference between a fish, or a missed bite.

During the night I use 6lb line, as this allows that extra confidence when playing fish in the dark; in the daylight, weed permitting, I will use 4lb. On the business end I like to ring the changes: perhaps a lobworm on a size 10 hook, or hair rigged maggots fished either with a running lead or bolt rig. Each new season I find that a slight variation may be needed to catch, either in presentation or bait.

Together with my leger weights I carry a number of leger sticks which vary in weight and length. On the top of the stem I attach a small, flat circular collar of plastic, trimmed to counter the weight of the lead. This is used so the leger will sink at a controlled speed – the idea being to allow the leger weight to sink into the silt, leaving the collar lying flat on top of it. This allows the top of the stick to stand proud, and the line can lie on top of the silt (Diagram 40). Using a short hooklink of 2 or 3 inches, I fish these rigs tight to the back of the swim. Another useful method has been to fish maggots as pop-ups. Both ploys have accounted for fish when more orthodox methods have failed.

A good set of waterproofs is essential: fishing from a punt in open water leaves you exposed to the elements, and I well remember one session when it rained non stop for fifteen hours. I do use an umbrella, but find it hinders me at the best of times. To secure it I use an angle bracket which is clamped to the punt; it consists of two 'U'-shaped pieces of metal pop-riveted to one face – the top bracket is just enough to take the umbrella, the bottom one traps the point. By clamping the bracket, it allows me to position the umbrella as I like.

When fishing I try to keep movement in the punt to a minimum, so it is important to sort out the tackle and bait so that everything is to hand. A good comfortable chair

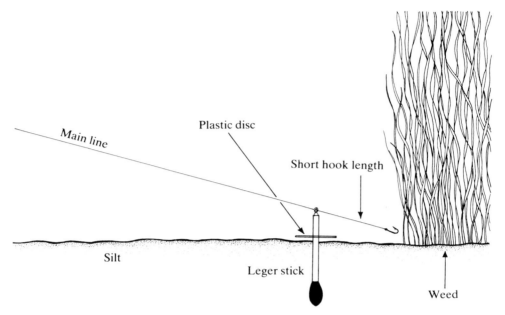

Diagram 40 Leger stick fished tight to the back of the swim

is essential, as night sessions can be up to fifteen hours long. I organise the punt so that my chair is positioned on a piece of polyurethane rubber, to prevent noise from the chair legs carrying through the bottom of the punt. I also wrap pipe-lagging around the anchor pole at the water line to muffle any noise should the punt bump against them. Finally for fish handling, I carry a piece of foam rubber to lay the fish on while unhooking; this protects it from damage.

Why fish from a punt and not from the bank? Many times have I heard the lads fishing the bank swims complain that they were only having twitches, or that they had lost a big fish. Considering that they were fishing 80 yards out in dense weed, this is hardly surprising. However, out in the boat I feel more in touch with the fish, and can easily adjust my tactics to suit conditions. Being at a relatively short distance I am able to convert those twitch bites, and when playing a fish I have more control – in fact, I can even stand on the centre seat of the punt with the rod held high to gain more control. At 80 yards, bank anglers have only one angle of pull.

At times I will see fish approaching the swim – not topping or throwing up clouds of bubbles, but just the slightest of signs, and I can be ready to convert the slightest dip of the float by being on the rod. I can loose feed, which can only be beneficial. And last but not least, I do not have to compete for a swim as those on the bank do and that allows me peace of mind.

Since I started fishing the Mere the tench have been getting progressively bigger, and I doubt that we have seen the best of this water yet. Hopefully, that elusive double will come my way – a particular ambition I got close to realising in 1987.

TENCH FISHING FROM A PUNT

The season promised to be a good one. All the preparation had been done, and the weed growth was still sparse enough to allow me to use 4lb line. During the build-up the week before, the regulars had met in the pub after pre-baiting, and as usual the conversations had centred on the prospects for the following week.

Expectations ran high (as they always do), but as the regulars know only too well, the water can be hard whatever the conditions, and the opening day especially has a reputation of being unproductive.

The season opened on a Tuesday, and as usual I had arranged to have that week off work. My plan was to fish every night, as hopefully that would give me the chance of a really big one.

I arrived in the early evening, allowing myself plenty of time to sort the boat out, as I always find the first session a bit chaotic. by 9pm all the necessary jobs had been completed and the punt was tied up to the scaffolding poles, with both rods set up for legering. The only remaining job was to bait up.

At 10pm I rowed over the swim and baited it heavily. Back on the anchor poles, I made the final adjustments to the extendable bank-sticks, made a couple of trial casts, and then sat back taking in the atmosphere and waiting for the start.

You don't need a watch at midnight, as the distant thud of the leads hitting the water from the bank swims will tell you the time. A few minutes later my own baits were cast, the left-hand rod with lobworm and the right-hand with maggot, one down either side of the swim.

At around 2am a bleep from the optonics warned that something was showing interest, and over the next hour three or four single bleeps from the Optonic on the maggot rod confirmed this suspicion. Then suddenly, with no hestitation, the isotope on the maggot rose to the butt. I struck into a solid resistance and held the pressure as the fish kited off to the right – I stood up to gain a little more control as it ran strongly past the end of the punt. This felt like a big one. I played it from the back of the boat, and after a couple more runs it was guided into the net.

As I lifted the net into the boat I guessed its weight at around 8½lb, but was delighted to record it at 9lb 14oz: not only a personal best, but the largest to date from the Mere.

After sacking the tench for photographing later, I fished on with the lead, but no further action took place. At first light I changed one of the rods over to the float, 4lb line, with double maggot on a size 16 hook. Then at 5.30am the float dipped and my strike was once again met with solid resistance. The fight which followed was the best scrap I have ever had from a tench; it took me in a full circle of the punt and went burrowing away from the net on two or three occasions. When I finally managed to scoop it out, it was a male fish weighing 6lb 7oz, another personal best. So who says the Mere does not fish the first day?!

Nevertheless the Mere *is* difficult at the best of times, even from the punt, so blanks must be expected, especially as the season progresses. Occasionally though there is a real red letter day.

TENCH FISHING FROM A PUNT

Sunday 24 June 1990 was one of them. Once again, conditions were perfect – in fact, the early season had given the most consistent fishing conditions I've known since I started fishing the Mere, with water temperatures registering a constant 61°F for the first two weeks.

The night failed to produce a bite, even though numerous tench had rolled both in and around the swim. At first light I changed both rods over to floats with 4lb line, one for maggots, the other for casters. And at 4.20am events began to change rapidly: my first bite came to the caster rod and resulted in a tench of 6lb 15oz; after rebaiting, I recast – and within seconds, was in again. This was another female weighing 6lb 15oz. With all the action coming to caster and not wanting to risk losing a fish by tangling the other rod, I wound that one in so I could concentrate on the caster rod.

Another fish soon followed, a male of 4lb 2oz, after which there was a quiet spell. Then at around 6.45am the float lifted once again and this time the strike met with what was obviously a far better fish: eventually I managed to slip the net under a beauty of 8lb 2oz. Once again all activity ceased, but I wasn't complaining! I'd had a good session with four tench, including another 'eight' of 8lb 13oz which I had taken the previous day.

However, there was more action to come: between 9.00 and 10.30am I landed a further five tench – three of those over 6lb – and lost another when the hook pulled out. One of these powered away under the punt while on its way to the net, diving straight through the scaffolding poles. This left me facing one way with the rod bent double and the tench visibly fighting away down in the water behind me. The only option seemed to be to plunge the landing net down in front of it, but this had the opposite effect and made it make a 180° 'U' turn back through the anchor poles and out into the swim again. I let her go, but made sure that her next introduction to the landing net went without mistakes!

The morning finished with a total of nine tench, weighing in at 6lb 12oz, 6lb 15oz, 4lb 2oz, 8lb 2oz, 6lb 8oz, 6lb 9oz, 6lb, 4lb 4oz and 5lb 12oz – all falling to casters. Truly a red letter day.

Barry Snape poses with the fruits of a real red-letter day

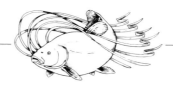

10

CHESHIRE MERE TENCH

Roger Harker

The meres of Cheshire have long been famous for their bream fishing. During the sixties and seventies these waters yielded many specimens, some in excess of 10lb, and were visited by anglers from all over the country in pursuit of a 'double' and in the faint hope of beating the record fish, which then stood at 13lb 8oz. The meres in those days constituted the 'Mecca' for bream anglers. It was during the late sixties that I started to fish these waters seriously, slowly gaining knowledge and developing techniques that eventually brought success with bream into double figures. Fishing for big tench was just not considered worth while. A few fish were caught while bream fishing, normally in the 3 to 4lb range, with the occasional fish around the 5lb mark. In truth there seemed to be very few fish and not particularly large. However, that was soon to change dramatically.

The Cheshire meres must have begun to evolve as big tench waters in 1975. The summer of 1975 was nearly as hot and dry as the famous drought year of 1976, and at this time I and my constant angling companion Eddie Bibby were fishing a small mere in south Cheshire for its bream. We'd had very little success in the hot still days of June and July; water levels were dropping alarmingly, and giant algae rafts were drifting slowly all over the mere. Very few fish were rolling which was a little worrying and most unusual on this water. Then on a Monday morning in August a phone call from Doug Sturney confirmed our worst suspicions. He had gone to fish that morning only to be confronted by dozens of bream in the 7 to 10lb range dead or dying in the margins. Later in the day we counted fifty dead bream, a few perch and rudd, and one tench. Results from water samples confirmed very low oxygen levels, and the bream being the largest species had suffered much more than others.

We did not return to fish the mere until four years later, but when we did, we were amazed at the situation we encountered.

As dawn broke on our first visit, the indicator on my left-hand rod leapt into the butt ring. The speed of this took me by surprise, and as the reel started backwinding I tightened into what felt very much like a tench. It was, and eventually weighed in at 4lb 8oz. This was to be the first of twenty tench that Ed and I caught, all before 11am when the bites ceased. The largest fish weighed 5lb 7oz. As far as I knew, that mere had never produced such a catch of tench before; in fact to catch one tench had

Dawn creeps over the Mere as anticipation mounts

been quite a rarity. Subsequent visits that season saw us take similar catches. It wasn't too difficult to guess what had taken place on this mere: as the bream had died in 1975, tench had filled the void and had obviously thrived, particularly with two extremely good spawning years in 1975 and 1976.

Strangely, the next couple of seasons saw several other Cheshire meres start producing big tench, and the grapevine was hot with news of 'sixes' and 'sevens' coinciding with the disappearance of bream shoals. This was explicable on the mere where we knew the bream had died, but we could see no reason in other waters where such a bream kill had not occurred – and at least six or seven waters had taken a very similar route since the mid-seventies. Moreover this seemed to be a nationwide trend, particularly in the south with 7lb, 8lb and incredibly 9lb tench hitting the headlines in the angling press, when just a few years earlier a 'six' was considered exceptional. Whatever the reasons, one thing was for certain: the early eighties heralded the start of serious big tench fishing on the once famous bream domains of Cheshire.

The early eighties saw Ed and me divide our time between bream and tench. The tench offered a realistic challenge from 16 June to mid-July depending on spawning, and again for a short spell in September, but to fish for them at other times spelled blank after blank, as they just seemed to disappear.

The beautiful meres of Cheshire vary in size from about 10 to 100 acres, and were formed as the ice retreated during the last ice age. They are generally reed-fringed with extensive shallow areas and depths not normally exceeding 20 feet. Some have a variety of features such as ledges, drop-offs and plateaux, whilst others have no contours at all and are simply bowl-like. The bottom can vary from firm sandy gravel to almost liquid, foul-smelling black mud. They are extremely rich in natural food such as daphnia, snails, shrimps, bloodworm and so on, and this, coupled with relatively low numbers of fish, provides an ideal environment for fish to reach their maximum potential.

One thing common to all these waters is their famous annual 'bloom', when – depending on weather conditions – algae forms in great clumps in the shallows and is them amassed into huge rafts which break away and roam with the wind to all corners of the water. This always seems to coincide with the start of the season, and as many of the rafts seem to end up in our neglected swim, the task of clearing it is extremely hard work indeed! However, it is this abundance of algae that is in fact so vital to success, particularly at this time of year.

In June 1985 Ed and I had an invitation from Dave and Carl, two good friends, to fish a strictly private mere of approximately 40 acres. As this water had produced a 9lb 8oz tench two years previously, we were naturally delighted. Again it turned out that here was another mere which had been an out-and-out bream and roach water until the mid-seventies, when tench also started to appear. Now it held only eels, pike and tench; so with hardly any competition for the vast riches of natural food available, the tench had grown very big indeed.

On our first visit we found only three accessible bankside points amongst the dense reedbeds. In some areas, huge beds of lilies stretched for yards, from the reeds to deeper water. It looked like a tench paradise, but where to begin?

We decided to row over the lake so as to find out as much about the bottom contours as possible. It soon became apparent that the shallows resembled a dense jungle of algae, and anywhere we might decide to fish would have to be cleared just to allow us to get near any likely-looking feature.

We began exploring the south bank in the early afternoon, and almost immediately found a ledge approximately 15 yards from the bank. It sloped from a few inches to about 7 feet and a further 5 yards out it dropped again to 14 feet. This looked very promising, particularly as a large tench rolled quite close to the boat. We stopped rowing and ran the boat into the reedbed to find a firm bit of ground on which to fish from. We decided to make one swim that would take both of us, and then set about clearing it. The reeds were quickly cut back and the next stage was to rake out the algae and weed so we could reach the first shelf.

Our rake weighs about 30lb and consists of six garden claw rakes welded to a piece of angle iron approximately 3 feet long; it had to be rowed out and lowered into the water and dragged back to the bank. The amount of weed it always brings in is unbelievable, but it still took about forty drags to make this swim fishable. We

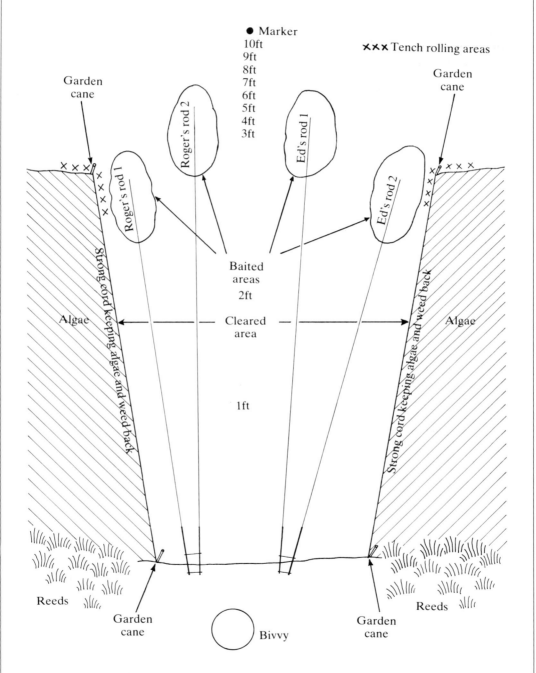

CHESHIRE MERE TENCH

● Marker
10ft
9ft
8ft
7ft
6ft
5ft
4ft
3ft

✗✗✗ Tench rolling areas

Garden cane

Garden cane

Roger's rod 2

Ed's rod 1

Roger's rod 1

Ed's rod 2

Baited areas
2ft

Cleared area

1ft

Strong cord keeping algae and weed back

Strong cord keeping algae and weed back

Algae

Algae

Reeds

Reeds

Garden cane

Garden cane

Bivvy

Diagram 41 Cleared tench swim on the mere

also decided to peg back the algae to stop it drifting into the clearing we had made. This we did by placing a bamboo cane at the edge of the algae, then tying a length of cord to this and to another cane on the bankside (Diagram 41).

Preparation of the swim had taken about four hours and as dusk was fast approaching, it was time to bait up. This consisted of 6lb of dry brown breadcrumb, 2 pints of hemp, 2 pints of maggots and caster and 2 tins of John West sweetcorn. This was deposited equally between the two drop-offs in 6 feet and 12 feet respectively. It was obvious that tackle would need to be fairly heavy with all the weed about, so rods were 11ft 6in, 1lb 10oz T.C. Conoflex Carbons; line strength was 6lb b.s. reel line to 5lb b.s. hooklinks, attached to ½ or ¾oz Arlesley bombs depending on wind conditions; and we decided on a double hook rig that we had developed in the seventies for breaming. This would be baited with corn and maggot and maybe a lobworm or breadflake (Diagram 42).

Doubling up would hopefully tell us the going bait more quickly. Once the bivvy was set up, we were ready to cast: we opted to put two baits on the near ledge and two on the far one; bobbins were clipped on and the rods placed on the Optonics, and we then slumped exhausted into our bed-chairs as the sun set. Tench were now rolling fairly often at the edge of the algae in the fast fading light. The breeze had almost died away and the air was heavy with expectancy. Fifteen minutes later, Eddie's bait on the near ledge was taken by a powerful fish which tore into the algae

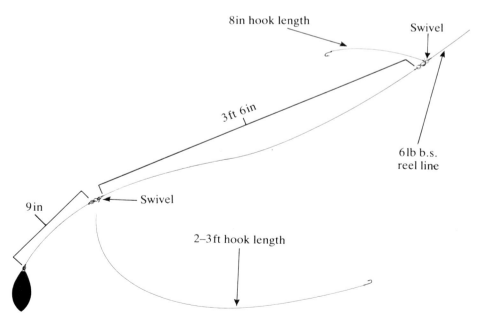

Diagram 42 Double-hook fixed paternoster rig

to his right and went solid. I waded as far as possible and began clearing algae with the landing net. Fortunately it worked, and a few minutes later a big female enveloped in a mass of weed was in the landing net. It weighed 7lb 6oz. The following morning I took a fish of 7lb 1oz, also on the near line. Both fish had taken two grains of sweetcorn on size 10 hooks.

We were well pleased: two superb fish on our first visit. Because we had found fish of such calibre so quickly, we didn't feel the need to look any further, which later proved to be a mistake. However, it was difficult to leave a swim which over the next two years produced a number of tench from 5½lb to just under 8lb. Moreover it would have been three years, but 1987 saw the water levels so high that access to the mere was impossible.

In early June 1988 we started clearing our first swim. The cold spring had held the algae and reeds back, however, and with little work to do we decided to drift slowly back up the lake in the late morning sunshine. The water was exceptionally clear and through our Polaroids we could easily see up to 10 feet down. We paddled close to the bank hoping to drift over fish; then halfway up the right-hand bank I suddenly found myself staring into darkness where before had been sandy gravel. We had discovered a steep drop-off only 8 yards from the bank – the ledge dropped to 10 feet in the space of 5 yards, and it simply screamed tench. We decided there and then to move swims at the start of the season in the hope of taking a really big fish.

We decided to adopt the same tactics that had proved successful in our other swim, not least remembering the importance that the floating algae had had in our catches – for the first few weeks of the season the tench just love the cover this floating mass provides. They would roll confidently on its fringes and, when we were either baiting up or landing a fish we would quite often disturb one that was resting up in it. It was most important when raking that only enough weed was removed to give a fair chance of landing a fish – to rake a swim bare had in the past produced far fewer bites. The rods Eddie and I had fished closer to the dense algae had noticeably outfished the other two; the fish had obviously felt more at ease the closer they were to their 'jungle' home, and would take a bait confidently.

Opening day soon saw us settled into our new swim. Our inside rods were cast halfway down the ledge in about 6 feet of water, the outside ones on top of it in only 2 feet 6 inches. Hookbaits were still corn and maggot. The best bait had proved to be two grains of corn, with four maggots on a size 12 hook coming second best, and worm a poor third. During that first weekend we took several fish to 7lb 11oz – but even more important, we saw two or three exceptional tench. One fish in particular

PAGE 135
Yorkshire expatriate Simon Lush returns an 8lb tench to its southern home

PAGE 136
(top) *Dave Cable, ex-member of the Eastbourne Hit Squad,
with an immaculate 9lb 2oz fish*
(below) *Anctication mounts on the opening morning of a new season on a new water*

took our breath away as it rolled just several yards out. On its first apperance I thought it was two fish, but as it rolled again I realised the dorsal and immense tail fin belonged to the same fish. The look on Ed's face confirmed it... truly a fish of which dreams are made.

We couldn't wait for the following weekend, and arrived early on the Friday afternoon; a quick raking and we were ready. We waited until early evening before baiting up, and cast out at about 7pm. It was a warm, slightly overcast June evening, with only a light cooling breeze out of the south gently rippling the surface. It seemed absolutely perfect. At about 9pm we saw a tench roll, followed by another in quick succession right over the baited area. The indicator flickered and twitched, indicating fish were about but as yet not taking the baits. (Yes, we had tried hitting the twitches but to no avail.)

It wasn't until about 2am that Ed's Optonic screamed into action. He struck into what seemed to be 'The Flying Scotsman' as it took about 20 yards of line on its first run. Was this the big one, we wondered? Unfortunately not, though it turned out to be a huge male fish of 6lb 12oz. We caught another four fish before dawn, then the bites ceased. This was most unusual, as I have never found darkness a good time for tench, either here or on other waters. First light to late morning is usually by far the best period.

The following evening saw us follow the same procedure. Then at 9.25pm a small twitch on my left-hand indicator developed into a steady pull to the butt ring. As I struck, the algae at 10 yards seemed to explode as a broad expanse of olive-green flank crashed through into the open water; the rod arched over and the line began singing in the breeze. I managed to confine the fight to the relatively clear water, and Ed was soon ready with the landing net. As the fish approached the net it made one final run for the 'jungle'; the water displacement on this terrific surge was quite spectacular and we both realised this fish was something special. I managed to stop it just before it reached the algae wall, and Ed put the net under it. It had taken two grains of corn on the bottom hook. Ed placed this magnificent fish into the weigh sling and turned the Avons away from me. The puzzled look on his face and the shaking of the scales to make sure they were weighing correctly had me wondering. He eventually turned the dial towards me, and I realised why: the needle was clearly reading 10lb 3oz. We couldn't believe it! A Cheshire 'double', and this time a tench; a few years earlier a fish of such size had seemed impossible, but now here it was, lying at our feet, undisputed proof that our beloved meres *were* capable of producing tench such as this.

Unfortunately the following year found the mere totally unfishable again – the exceptionally warm spring had seen the algae bloom so much that it was impossible to clear. However, the 1990 season was just one day old when unbelievably, I caught another 'double', this time weighing 10lb 1oz and taken on a single grain of corn. Oh, how the meres have changed since 1975!

I seriously believe there are now probably three meres in Cheshire and one in Staffordshire that could be challenging the record in the next few years. Ed and I will be trying even harder, that's for sure. You see, we can't forget that huge fish we saw a couple of years earlier. Yes, it was quite a bit bigger than our 'Cheshire tens'...

Roger Harker's second Cheshire double, this one weighing 10lb 3oz

Roger returning a massive 10lb 1oz to a private mere

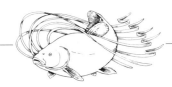

11

JOHNSONS' SCENARIOS

Chris Turnbull

Tench were always my favourite species. It was one of those feelings which grew with me from childhood when the desire to catch a really big one became rooted in my mind even then, and was pursued from one water to the next as I grew to adulthood. And over the years this ambition was raised and beaten, ounce by precious ounce, until my best, a fish caught from a Devonshire canal, eventually stood at 5lb 4oz.

It was a fish which at the time seemed huge, but it was soon to be pushed into insignificance by a wave of truly huge tench being caught in the south-east of the country. I remember looking with envy at photographs in *Coarse Fisherman* of Kevin Clifford and Steve Harper posing with Norfolk sevens. And in a book called *The Big Fish Scene*, I read Len Head's story of Bures Lake and the capture of fish to over 8lb. Fish like those were almost beyond belief, like inhabitants of a different planet.

You can therefore imagine my sense of anticipation when in 1979 circumstances led me to taking temporary residence in Kent, and I found myself standing on the banks of a fishery which had earned the reputation of being the best tench water in the country. Here, 5lb and 6lb tench were merely average, sevens were caught regularly, eights were the target and nines were becoming a distinct possibility. Other waters produced bigger fish, but none could compare with the numbers of big fish being caught here at Johnsons.

Johnsons consists of three lakes, available on day and season tickets, all of which hold numbers of big tench and carp. The lakes are firstly the Pub Lake, a mature 30-acre pit named after its close proximity to the local watering hole; secondly the Island Lake, an island-strewn pool of perhaps a third of that size which is joined to the Pub Lake by a narrow channel; and last but not least, the Railway Lake, a very deep pit of about 12 acres. Each pit is characteristically different from the other, but all share the quality of being rich, clear and weedy, making them ideal big fish waters – and indeed, over the years, they have produced big fish of many species. Since the mid-seventies however, it is the carp and tench which have dominated these lakes and made them nationally renowned.

A power-packed 8lb 9oz taken on 3lb line which proved a real test for my nerves

They were amongst the first waters to be effectively tackled by Fred Wilton and friends when he was developing his HNV approach to baiting. Not surprisingly therefore they were also the place where modern carp-fishing approaches to catching tench were first adopted.

For my own part, I had precious little experience of boilies, bolt rigs and the like, when I planned my first sessions on the lakes. Over the years all that would change, but for the time being I would stick with the time-honoured approaches which had worked for me in the past.

As 16 June slowly approached during the summer of 1980, I made constant visits to the lakes and spent time both plumbing and fish-spotting. In early June I became aware of numerous tench and carp gathering along the deep weedy marginal shelf along one bank of the Railway Lake. There and then a pre-baiting plan was hatched, and the following morning at six o'clock I was back at the lake with half a gallon of stewed wheat; I intended to bait an area less than two rod-lengths out, where 10 feet down a small gravel hump visibly emerged from the Canadian pondweed.

The same procedure was carried out each morning for the following week, then stepped up to twice daily for a few days before the opening. Each visit found the previous baiting had gone, and very often I was privileged to watch as first the tench and later the carp gathered to clear up my offerings. The plan was working, and so it was with great excitement and anticipation that I settled into the swim on the evening of the fifteenth.

After tackling two light hollow glass Avons with 5lb line, running link legers and size 8 Mustad hooks, I introduced two pints of wheat to the hump and sat back to await the magic hour. Up to now I had rarely seen any other anglers on the bank, but soon most of the swim became occupied. By half-past-eight, the air seemed electric with expectancy, and this was enhanced by the sight of a group of tench grazing on my offerings.

The bailiff was doing his rounds and I was amazed to see several anglers already casting out without being reprimanded. As dusk settled in, I watched incredulously as an angler in one of the causeway swims played a good tench to the net. I gradually realised that it was only myself and a few others who were playing by the rules, and for the first and only time in my life, I cast in before midnight. How things change with the passing years; there I sat, feeling guilty yet bursting with anticipation – I only wish I could retain that level of enthusiasm today.

Within minutes of placing my baits, as I strained my eyes to see the tench feeding in the gathering gloom, my nearside rod-top nodded a fraction. I hesitated, expecting the bobbin to climb: but that was it, my chance had gone, and apparently so had the tench.

After an uneventful night, I rebaited the swim and waited patiently; as the light grew, I became slowly aware of vague shapes moving and tilting over my baits. I turned my attention back to the rods, and this time when the rod-tip flickered I struck without hesitation: the rod arched as my opponent powered down through the long fronds of milfoil which curtained the bottom of the shelf. The battle was short but spirited, and soon I was able to draw the fish over the net. At 6lb exactly, she christened what was to become a long and fruitful relationship with some remarkable waters.

Over the next week I made three more visits to the Railway, each lasting the afternoon and evening. The first recorded a blank, the second a thirty-minute struggle with a superb leather carp of 25lb 2oz, and the third, a brace of tench with the bigger of the two also weighing 6lb exactly. I was delighted with these successes, but nevertheless disappointed that few of the tench being caught by myself or others seemed much over 6lb. However, news from the Pub Lake was much more encouraging, with many sevens being landed during opening week. In about a week I was due to move to Norfolk, and so had little time to get to grips with the lake; however, now that the crowds of bivvies were thinning out, my chance to move in had come.

The swim which had taken my fancy during pre-season visits was quite different to the one on the Railway; it consisted of a very pronounced drop-off about 60 yards out from the bank, and obviously totally different tactics were called for.

My first session in that swim will stand out for ever in my mind. It was one of those beautiful, calm summer dawns when the surface of the lake perfectly reflected the surroundings like a mirror; but as I prepared my tackle, it became broken by the dimpling of small roach and fry, interspersed by numerous rolling tench and regularly punctuated by the noisy crashes of big carp. Never before or since have I seen so much fish activity, and I can still vividly remember actually trembling with excitement.

I mixed a large bowl of crumb with a pint of wheat, a pint of maggots and half a can of sweetcorn, and then catapulted twenty balls to the slopes of the drop-off area before casting out my baits. Both rods were rigged with 10in buoyant stick legers and 3ft long 5lb b.s. hooklinks. A big feederlink and three maggots on a size 14 hook were assigned to one rod, and two grains of sweetcorn on a size 8 to the other. Both rods were equipped with swingtips; after my experiences on the Railway Lake I was expecting twitches.

With so much activity showing on the water I was half expecting some instant action, but this was not to be, and four biteless hours passed as the sun climbed high in the sky and reflected awkwardly on the water right between my swingtips. The fish had stopped rolling now, it was seven o'clock, and a gentle breeze began to ruffle the surface. Having just recast the feeder rod to top up the swim, I sank the line and had barely placed the rod in its rests when the swingtip lurched out straight. I struck hard but missed it. The maggots were untouched; maybe it was a line bite. Ten minutes later it was a different story as the tip pulled out straight once again. This time the strike met with solid resistance – but as the fish powered off, the hook pulled out.

I rebaited and cast the feeder to the baited area, and just as I put it in the rests, the tip on the sweetcorn rod whipped up parallel and the reel handle began to churn. So much for twitches. I struck and held on as my adversary moved ponderously out into deeper water. No rocket this, just an unyielding force, but slowly I gained some line and eventually had her back up the shelf and wallowing in the shallow water. Five minutes later the net buckled as I hoisted my prize from the water; my target had been a seven, so imagine my jubilation when the dial settled at 8lb exactly!

There followed a succession of bites to the feeder rod: one I missed, the second pulled off (remember what I said about small hooks on p27?), and the third (after changing to a size 12) resulted in a 4lb 7oz male.

For the following two visits – one made in the morning and one in the evening – I used the same tactics in the same swim, and this resulted in a string of fish over 5lb, including a 6lb 13oz, a 6lb 4oz and a spawn-filled female of 7lb 10oz.

After moving to Norfolk, I continued to fish Johnsons as often as time permitted, at first on my own and later accompanied by Suffolk angler Jim Bigden. Together we worked at developing new approaches to our fishing: we adopted boilies, self-hooking rigs and hair rigs, and gradually our tally of big tench increased. Jim especially enjoyed success with many fish over 8lb, his best being a superb 25½in long creature weighing 9lb 7oz. I had several 'sevens' both from this and other waters, but any fish larger than my first eight-pounder totally eluded me. Up to this point our efforts at Johnsons had all been directed to the Pub Lake. I wanted to move on, the Railway Lake fish were coming on in leaps and bounds and I felt drawn to the challenge of a new water. The only thing stopping me was the notion that the Pub Lake owed me a really big fish.

Jim Bigden with the first of many 9s that we caught at Johnson's

As the 1986 season approached we made our plans for another assault on the water. This would be my last, it would be big fish or bust. Jim went down several days before the start. He had set his sights on the gap, a swim which incorporated the lake's main spawning area, and he knew he would have to get there early if he was to claim the swim. I was unable to get down before the 15th, and little did I know how thin the choice of the remaining swims would be. I travelled down overnight in the company of Norwich angler John Sadd and arrived before dawn, but a quick scan confirmed the worst of my fears: all the swims with any early season consistency were taken. However, I hoped my detailed knowledge of the lake, gained through experience, could make the best of a bad situation. The swim I chose was known as the stables and used to be quite popular, but water levels had risen by six feet when pumping had stopped on the nearby Larkfield pit, and since then it had become over-grown from neglect.

The swim itself (Diagram 43, Fig 1) covered the end of a long, shallow, willow-covered gravel bar which ran parallel to the bank and ended 80 yards to my left at the gap where Jim and Simon Lush were entrenched. It was an area which I knew the tench would use for spawning, but which offered few weed-free areas in which to place the rigs. Nevertheless, I felt confident that I could extract a few fish from it.

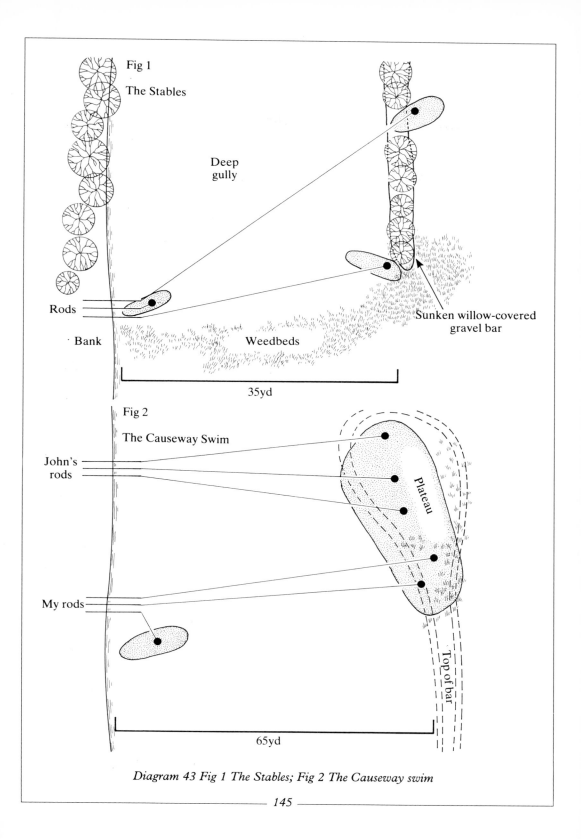

Fig 1

The Stables

Deep
gully

Rods

Bank

Weedbeds

Sunken willow-covered
gravel bar

35yd

Fig 2

The Causeway Swim

John's
rods

Plateau

My rods

Top of bar

65yd

Diagram 43 Fig 1 The Stables; Fig 2 The Causeway swim

After a few hours' careful exploration, a plan was hatched. I would use three rods, one cast a little to the left through a narrow gap in the willows to land on a weed-free gravel patch on the back of the bar; so I could quickly bully hooked fish back through the willow roots, this rod was equipped with 11lb Sylcast. The middle rod would be cast to the end of the bar to land on its nearside shelf on a gravel patch between a thick bed of milfoil and the silt bed at the bottom of the bar. Both of these spots would be baited with boilies. The third rod would be baited with corn and dropped into the margins in a small open area between a bed of submerged reeds and a patch of sparse milfoil.

As midnight approached, we sat chatting in the gap swim watching the endless stream of tench rolling in the hotspot. It was well past twelve when I got back to my swim; I had been awake for two days and was dead on my feet. It was too dark to make any accurate casts to the bar, but I placed them as close as I dared and dropped the corn rod into the margin, supported by a handful of corn, and turned in for a few hours of desperately needed sleep.

The tench at Johnsons rarely feed actively at night, so when the margin rod Optonic beeped once or twice in the dark I took little notice, putting it down to the antics of little roach hiding out in the milfoil. However, just before dawn the same buzzer suddenly screamed out with unmistakeable urgency.

The tussle which followed was spirited but short lived, as I hassled my captive into the waiting net. Having removed the hook, I was tempted to return the fish without putting it through the indignity of weighing. It's funny what tiredness can do, and the size of the fish hadn't sunk in, but as I slipped down the bank with it I suddenly became aware of its bulk and decided to weigh it after all. It was just as well I did, because at 9lb 0½ oz it represented a new milestone in my career!

The rest of the week exceeded all expectations and put the stables back on the map as an exceptional swim. I don't remember how many fish I caught; I know twelve weighed over 5lb with three of these over 7lb, including a massive male of 7lb 2½ oz.

So ended my involvement with the Pub Lake. The following season was to begin on the Railway; although it held only low numbers of tench, it had now begun to produce some very big fish including a double of 10lb 1oz to carp angler Keith Furgusson. Once again this session was to be spent in the company of John Sadd, and we arrived at the water a little after 2am on 15 June.

After watching the water for a while, our attention was repeatedly drawn to an area of activity where both tench and carp rolled regularly, 70 yards out from the causeway separating the Railway from Leisure Sport's Larkfield Pit. Further investigation revealed that the two swims commanding this area were unoccupied, so we quickly claimed them.

There was much to prepare; after setting up the bivvies, we blew up the inflatable dinghy and set to work charting the swim. John worked over the area with an echo sounder, while I plumbed from the back and felt for weed. Together we defined a

My first ' 9'; 9lb 0½oz, and nearly returned without weighing

large plateau on John's side, which tapered off into a very pronounced razor of a bar in front of my swim and ran for 100 yards up the lake (Diagram 43, Fig 2). This corresponded exactly with the area of fish activity we had observed in the night.

After setting out the markers, an area incorporating both the plateau and part of the top and nearside bottom of the bar was then baited with a gallon of wheat and two mixes of ultra-spice boilies. Our plan was to hold as many fish as possible and test the going from there on. I also baited a smaller area at the bottom of the marginal shelf with a smaller quantity of wheat and boilies for a third rod.

Just after dawn on opening morning I missed an absolute flier on the rod positioned on the top of the bar, but a few hours later struck another which yielded a mirror of 21½lb. With such a large amount of bait out there, we knew there was a risk of attracting carp, and that this could push the tench off the baits, but for a day or two we would run that risk.

The rest of opening day was fairly quiet. Early in the afternoon we rebaited with a similar amount of feed, and at tea-time my marginal rod produced a male tench of 6lb 7oz.

The following morning was cold, wet and dismal, and all around the lake hardly a soul strayed from the confines of the bivvies. It had been a long time since there was any sign of fish activity, so it was a surprise when, at 6.30am, the monkey on the rod positioned on top of the bar slid in a flurry of spray to the top of the needle. I half ran, half slid to the rod, and bent into a slowly kiting fish which gradually took line then dropped down and weeded up solid at the back of the bar. Luckily the weed wasn't too dense and after a while I had the fish on the move again. For a while she came quietly with weed over her eyes, but as she approached the bank in mid-water the weed came free, so we battled it out in open water.

John stood ready with the submerged net and we both gasped at her bulk as I pumped her to the surface. On the bank it was difficult to guess her weight; at $22\frac{1}{2}$ in she wasn't long, but she was broad and carrying a fair amount of spawn. For a moment or two we suspected she might be a double, but the scales revealed her true weight at 9lb 8oz.

In fact this was the only tench to come from the heavily baited area that week, and my fears that the carp might push them out were confirmed when John took a succession of three twenties up to $28\frac{1}{2}$lb. The marginal swim however, proved good for a couple of days, with tench of 8lb 7oz and 7lb 4oz; then it, too, dried up. The rest of the session was inconclusive with the fish becoming progressively more uncooperative, though I was lucky enough to have a further two fish weighing 8lb 14oz and 8lb 5oz.

Between Jim, Simon and myself, that opening session provided no less than six nine-pounders and eleven eights, which is remarkable fishing by any standard; so when the following season came around, nothing could keep me away from Johnsons.

Unfortunately the fishing on the Railway was to become increasingly pressured from now on. Leisure Sport Angling had clamped down on its carp waters at Darenth and banned several anglers for a multitude of sins, from leaving rods unattended right through to solvent abuse. Not surprisingly, a number of these refugees had headed south to Johnsons, drawn by the prospects of big carp. Before long they would be joined by other refugees from further afield, including those banned from Longfield and Savey.

It was obvious that if we were to stand a chance of getting on fish, we would have to get there a few days early. This time I would be fishing with Jim, who by now had also had his fill of the Pub Lake and fancied a change of scenery.

Despite arriving early, many of the best swims were already occupied and so we decided to double up in the same swim, the one which had produced my 'nine' the previous season.

Our plan of action was to go all out with a heavy baiting of maggots fished from the margins, to as far out as we could loose feed them. We felt confident that this would preoccupy a large number of tench and keep them feeding in the swim.

This appeared to be highly successful, as for the next seven nights the swim positively heaved with tench, all in a frenzy to mop up the bait, the bobbins jerking all the while in response to the line bites. And yet one little problem stopped us cleaning up: despite constant experimentation with rigs – long and short hooklinks, sensitive rigs, bolt rigs, small hooks, hair rigs and all the rest – we struggled like idiots. By the end of the week, all we had to show for our efforts was one 'five', a 'six' and a few eels.

Eventually I could take the torment no longer, and as soon as a free swim appeared on the car park bank I rushed in there. The swim in question is a super early season swim, in fact probably the best on the lake. It consists of a marginal shelf which compared to the steep drop-offs which surround most of the lake, slopes gradually, and along which the tench tend to patrol between bouts of spawning.

After the failure of our heavy mass-baiting plan, I deemed it wise to adopt a little-and-not-very-often approach, consisting of a few pouches of maggots and a few samples of sweetcorn. My intention was to top up the swim only once a day, or after catching a fish, or after noticeable activity had died off in the swim regardless of whether I got bites or not.

The fishing remained painfully slow, but enough fish showed in the swim to prove they were interested, and over the next five days the bobbins lifted seven times. One was missed, one was the most manky 7lb bream that ever lived and one was the smallest carp in the lake; but the others made it all worth while, tench of 6lb 15oz, 6lb 15½oz, 8lb 9oz and finally a beautiful 25in creature weighing 9lb 7oz. As for Jim, he had to make do with an extremely angry 8lb 10oz tench foul-hooked in the vent.

The following season (1989/90) was to be our last at Johnsons. Jim, Simon and myself all agreed that the pressure on the waters was too much for us and our ultimate goal of a double was just not happening; Keith Furgusson's was still the only authenticated double to be taken. True, the fish were still inching up ounce by ounce and sooner or later it would happen, but we were losing our enthusiasm for the place. We all needed a totally new challenge. Idealism was creeping in, and we wanted to leave the crowded downtrodden banks and find a new water with unknown but massive potential, and to catch fish which had never been caught before. We were scouring the country to find our Utopia; many waters looked good, but were still not quite what we were looking for.

Our last season was spent together on the Railway where we were joined once again by John. The fishing was predictably slow – the fish had seen it all before. Nonetheless we still managed to put a few on the bank, with the highlight being an immaculate 9lb 11oz fish to Jim, which turned out to be my 9lb 7oz fish from the previous season.

The following season we found our Utopia: opening day found us immersed in splendid isolation on a huge expanse of water. What we caught is still on the official secrets list. However, when news filtered down the grapevine from Johnsons, we were not surprised to hear of two doubles weighing 10lb 10oz and 10lb 6oz. But for us our Johnsons' days were over.

12

THE LONG LIFE PIT

Len Arbery

Exactly when there was water there for the first time I don't know. It is said that during the years of World War II a rather insignificant pond of less than an acre existed on the site. Even then it apparently produced tench, but none of sufficient size to warrant the use of a landing net. After peace was finally restored it was changed for ever, like so many other ponds on the fringes of big cities. At this time England was repairing the damage caused by the ravages of war, and industry had a much freer hand than it has today – one reason was that materials, so necessary for the rebuild, were in very short supply. Today we would probably import them, but in those dark days of the early post-war years Britain was more self-sufficient and self-reliant, and I don't think the cost to the environment was even considered. Well, not for very long, anyway!

At least two big companies had set covetous eyes on the site containing the pond: because it was situated in the Colne Valley, an area rich in sand and gravel, one company wanted to excavate the aggregates there. The other, a local firm producing asbestos products, needed somewhere to dump its considerable amount of waste. Evidently the local council of the time recognised it could capitalise on this, and proposed that first, the gravel company could excavate the site, then the asbestos company's refuse could fill the resulting hole.

This, then, is an outline of the forces at work which culminated in the forming of the water we now know as the Long Life Pit. Long Life isn't its real name, of course; this title was derived from the body which controls the water, Long Life Angling Society, whose members have leased and controlled the water continually since those early days. Their influence has been most effective, and all those unsung heroes behind the scenes deserve our sincere thanks – the officers of the club who cheerfully carry out the club's tasks and who so often get only castigation in return. Gentlemen, without your efforts it wouldn't matter how good an angler was, for there would be no fish to catch, and no preserved water on which to angle! You have made it possible for many anglers' dreams to come true, especially those who specialise in catching very big tench.

Long Life Angling Society actually controls two pits, Troy and North Troy. These, as already mentioned, are situated in the Colne Valley and although adjacent to each other, have the River Colne flowing between them. Both the waters contain big tench, not discounting other species of course, but the account which follows will apply to North Troy, unless particularly specified otherwise. North Troy is also known as the 'Carpark Lake', and is the water the specialist angling world knows and reveres as simply 'Long Life'.

Way back in 1977 Bill Quinlan and I were fishing other Colne Valley waters for carp. The Long Life Pit was just down the road from one favourite haunt, and we often wondered if it, too, contained big carp. One hot and still morning after a night's carp fishing I spent some time walking around Long Life, and it was no great surprise to find three big carp all together in one bay.

At that time Bill and I had more carp fishing available than we could manage, so we 'filed' the information for possible future use. Roger Smith, however, lived out of the area and couldn't get on these other Colne Valley carp lakes, so when told about the carp I'd seen, he lost no time in joining Long Life (Roger's fishing club subscriptions over this period totalled more than my earnings!). Hence Roger became the first member of our little group, the Herts-Chiltern Anglers, to fish at Long Life.

It soon became apparent to Roger that my sighting of the carp had been a 'one-off' event – in fact for a long time afterwards most of our group, including me, thought I had been dreaming on that first visit, although much later, the carp *were* seen again. What Roger did discover on those early sorties was the existence of the tench. In those days a diary was kept by the members in the club hut; this contained all notable fish caught, and as they were eligible for prizes, each capture had to be witnessed. And it was of special and significant interest that the tench caught showed a significant weight gain each succeeding season. This meant only one thing to Bill and me: Long Life was an improving water and doubtless its best was yet to come. This situation was in direct contrast to most of the waters we were fishing at that time; some of these were a mere shadow of what they had been, producing fish only a fraction of the weight of the specimens they had produced in the past.

With an eye to the future, Bill, Bob Buteux and I all joined the Long Life Angling Society. Because of other tench-fishing commitments, however, quite a few seasons slipped past before we seriously took up the Long Life Challenge. Each of us had had previous 'flirtations' with the tench there of course, but the results were nothing remarkable. However, that was all about to change in June 1982.

I was away until 17 June but went over to the lakes as soon as possible to learn how my friends were doing. Bill was fishing the Carpark Lake from near the Silver Birch, halfway up the arm and Bob was fishing the Troy Lake. Neither had had much success, but Bob reported that another angler, fishing 20 yards or so to his left, had caught a tench of 8lb 12oz! This was an almost unbelievable weight for those days, so I just had to go and investigate. I wasn't surprised to learn that this was Mick Voller, an angler who has caught countless big fish over the years. What did surprise me was that he was about to pack up. When I'd cleared it with Mick – an essential precaution! – it was decided to fish his successful pitch. First, however the tackle and bait had to be collected from home, a task which was accomplished in record time. Why no speed cop apprehended me is a mystery! Anyway, all went well and Bob soon brewed a cup of tea to calm the nerves on my return.

On one rod we chose the same method and bait that Mick had been using: swim-feedered maggot fished two rod-lengths out. Fishing the same area, the other rod was baited with sweetcorn. At a quarter-past-midnight a bite on the corn rod produced a bream of 7lb 10oz. Not a bad start, but not what I'd come for, I needn't have worried though, for at 5am the lake yielded its first-ever tench for me, on the maggot rod; it weighed 5lb 2oz. A two-hour lull followed then two more tench both took the sweet-corn offering weighing in at 6lb 14oz and 7lb 1oz! Bob was steadily catching tench as well, but started complaining about the luck I was having. However you should have seen his face an hour later when he weighed my next tench ... 8lb 1oz! Although she was so ripe the spawn was pouring out of her, the memory of her will long burn in my mind's eye, for this was my first-ever eight-pounder. Maggot accounted for this fish, and also for my final tench of the morning, which weighed 5lb 7oz. So for my first-ever session on Troy, the average weight of these tench was an incredible 6lb 8oz! To put this fact in perspective, the average weight of the tench caught from Southill Park, arguably the number one tench lake of the sixties and seventies was around 5lb.

My first 7lb-plus tench therefore came from the Carpark Lake in the middle of a sunny Saturday afternoon in August 1982. Bait was breadflake, and the capture of this fish was remarkable not for the terrific fight it put up, but because it was the first I'd ever caught using the hair rig! Bill and I were covertly experimenting with the 'hair', trying to get a larger proportion of big tench bites, rather than the minute twitches we were constantly suffering.

Don't be misled, however, into believing that catching tench which give only small bites isn't both enjoyable and satisfying. I can sit all day, and half the night as well if necessary, and hardly take my eyes from my swingtips. Other tench anglers have laughed at how hard I fish at such times, but this is surely up to me, if I enjoy fishing in this manner? My fishing time is necessarily limited, hence I don't want to miss any opportunity to catch.

Of course, there are those who categorically state that tench don't give minute bites. Or, if they do, it's because the tackle or tactics employed are too heavy, or are incorrect. Nothing could be further from the truth; tench anglers who *only* get big, sailaway bites are either extremely fortunate, or just haven't recognised the twitch bites that have occurred! Anyway, if tench don't give small bites, why do so many successful tench anglers employ the most sensitive bite detection yet devised – the float? There are many reasons for a fish to give only a small bite, but I think they can be summed up by one word - wariness. Very often a new bait, or a new method will produce big bites but this happy situation will not last long. The tench will soon wise up, and you will be back to trying to deal with the small bite problem.

There is one particular method of bite indication that allows very small bites to be discerned, but in no way hinders a big sailaway bite should it occur. This method has proved so successful in coming to terms with big tench, that many of the anglers at Long Life (as well as elsewhere) have changed over to it.

The main feature is a swingtip, and you need to use a pair of rods thus equipped so you can compare the movement of one with the other. Originally, I had thought that the longer the tips, the more sensitive they would be, but this just isn't so. The maximum length that retains sufficient sensitivity and does not prove too difficult to cast with is about 18 inches. For lightness coupled with strength carbon fibre swingtips must be unbeatable. The hinge is a suitable diameter, 1 1/2 in length of silicon rubber tubing. Different stiffnesses are available to cope with the amount of undertow present, or to suit other conditions that affect the tips' behaviour. In very strong winds, a rod rest, say, positioned each side of each tip, can stop them flailing about too much.

For use after dark it is a simple matter to fit isotopes to swingtips; and narrow bands cut from silicon rubber tube, for example, will hold them securely. So as not to ruin the swingtips' sensitivity keep the betalights as small as possible, and for the same reason, take them off in daylight. Swingtips *are* so sensitive because they are in the right place, *ie* in front of the rod. There is no question of friction through the rod rings alarming a taking fish.

To ensure you can discern the slightest movement of your swingtip, it must be positioned accurately and correctly. You are trying to see a movement as little as 1/2 in (3mm) or less so you must have something against which to compare the movement of the tip. Therefore the tips must be just – and only just – touching the water; then if one or other of them lifts by even the merest fraction, you will see that movement immediately – providing, of course, that you haven't let your concentration waver, and looked away for some reason or another.

One final word: where big and perhaps wary tench are concerned, swingtipping isn't an easy option, but it can be recommended unreservedly. In one morning, for example, four tiny bites were connected with, and each produced a tench in excess of 7lb. I doubt if those bites could have been dealt with so successfully had I been using any other method! And that was by no means an isolated incident.

I again missed the start of the season in 1983 and didn't begin tench fishing until 20 June. Troy Lake was almost deserted because, I suspect, the fishing was so hard; in four days I only noticed about a dozen bites, most being small indications on the swingtip. Of these, nine produced tench: the smallest weighed 5lb 9oz and four were 'sevens'! All bites were on corn – the maggots proved useless, and I've no idea why.

As a postscript, in July of that year, Kevin Clifford and Mally Roberts fished as our guests. This was Kevin's first, and it turned out very nearly last, visit to Long Life: there was a plague of small but hard-biting black flies on the water that summer, and most of them picked on Kevin!

The start of the 1984 tench campaign was eagerly anticipated, but proved an anticlimax for me: the whole of the first week was spent fishing Troy, and produced just one five-pounder! Bill, though, was catching a few from the pitch in the Carpark

Ron Chant swingtipping from the 'point' at Long Life

Lake where the previous summer he had caught a brace weighing 7lb 13oz and 8lb 6oz, the latter fish having been his first eight-pounder. After some discussion, we decided to switch swims for the remainder of the summer, and concentrate our efforts on one situated at the end of an arm which almost divides the lake in two. Here, we deduced, the tench *must* pass when travelling from one main area of water to the other, and was surely an ideal place in which to ambush them. There were other advantages, too, not the least being that the channel joining the waters was narrow enough to concentrate the fish, yet wide enough to prevent other anglers from troubling us from the opposite bank. The main disadvantage was that the end of the arm was covered in stinking black mud, which stuck like glue to everything it touched, and was the breeding ground for the lake's mosquito population!

On Friday evening, 22 June, Bill and I set up on the end of the arm in preparation for a weekend's stay. We both chose to fish swimfeedered maggot, with bite detection on our trusty swingtips. We didn't have long to wait, and I was lucky enough to catch the first tench, a female weighing 5lb 14oz. Then it was action all the way until about 11pm when the fish stopped feeding. Nevertheless we were up at dawn, and it seemed they had been waiting for us; by the end of that day we'd taken more than twenty specimen-sized tench between us! On Sunday there was a repeat performance at dawn. Even so, at mid-morning Bill packed up to go home, as originally planned. I remained at the lake, however, eventually staying for the week, during which a stack of big tench were caught – the biggest of these weighed 8lb 10oz and was a personal best at the time.

Not surprisingly the tench became difficult to tempt after this onslaught, so I went carp fishing with Ron Chant and Bill went to the pub!

Bill dropped by to see us at the carp lake one Sunday morning. During the conversation he mentioned that a tench had been caught on a boilie from Long Life. So Bill and I made arrangements there and then to make a return to tench fishing the following weekend, and spent the intervening week baiting up the 'end of the arm' pitch with boilies.

Rather than make our own baits, we decided to try out the frozen Richworth boilies that had recently been introduced. Initially we were concerned that with a diameter of 16mm, these baits might have been too big for tench; but events were soon to prove our fears unfounded. On arrival at the lake for that first 'boilie sortie' Bill and I used two rods each as usual; one was baited with a boilie, the other with one of our conventional baits – sweetcorn or maggots – so we could compare the effectiveness of each bait.

I was the first to cast out, and the bait on this rod was a Salmon Supreme flavoured boilie. Before I had filled the feeder on my other rod, a tench was doing its best to pull the first one in! Weighing 4lb 10oz, its capture answered several nagging doubts: first and foremost, Long Life tench would indeed pick up baits of at least 16mm diameter; they would also accept boilies as food; the boilie mounted on a version of the hair rig had produced a sailaway bite; and further, the tench would accept a boilie mounted on a hair of the same strength as our main line, in this instance 4lb b.s.

During August and September 1984 Bill and I shared magnificent tench fishing: we caught more than one hundred tench between us, many over 6lb, along with several seven-pounders and two 'eights' – Bill's was 8lb 10oz and mine was just an ounce heavier, new personal bests for both of us.

After such success we awaited the 1985 season with great impatience. Two more friends had been invited to join in the fun, Ron Chant and Kevin Clifford. Ron and I lived nearest to Long Life and so carried out the pre-baiting, and as reward, had first choice of swims. After this close-season pre-baiting programme with Richworth

Len proudly displays this magnificent 8lb 11oz August-caught fish

boilies, I believe we had virtually every fish in the lake in our vicinity by the start of the season, and our results certainly seemed to confirm this belief!

Between us we caught no fewer than forty-three tench weighing over 7lb each in the first weeks of the season! What is more, some of them were exceptional fish: Kevin caught the first-ever 7lb male tench from Long Life, and Bill had eight tench over 8lb, seven of which were over 9lb, the heaviest at 9lb 7oz. Kevin had had to sit through what must have been a very difficult spell for him, when the three of us were catching and he was not, but typically he made up for it ... First he caught a 9lb 6oz fish, then a remarkable brace the next day of 9lb 10oz and 8lb 2oz, and finally took four fish over 9lb during this particular period. Bill, who considered himself chairman, secretary and president of the 'Nine Catchers' Club', at last grudgingly admitted me to membership of this illustrious body when I caught a tench of exactly 9lb. And Ron, in no way to be outdone, hoisted the lake record to 9lb 15oz, a target we still hope, however, to surpass from Long Life.

In subsequent seasons the Long Life tench inevitably wised up to our usual hair/bristle rig combination. As they did so, the rig's effectiveness diminished, and so did the big sailaway bites associated with it. As a result, Bill Quinlan and I found ourselves back to square one – trying to deal with microscopic bites. Then news reached us through the big-fish world's grapevine, that some of the top carp-boys had something new in rigs which was accounting for many massive carp from some of the country's most difficult waters – waters subject to considerable angling pressure, where the carp, like the Long Life tench, had learned to discriminate against all hair rig variations. This 'something new' was the now better known 'bent-hook' rig, and Bill and I resolved to try it out on the tench.

After much research and development, the best hook we found for the job was the Drennan Carbon Lure Hook. It comes in a wide range of sizes and can be acquired from any good tackle shop that caters for game-fishermen. It can be bent into the required shape by holding the shank in pliers, and using finger pressure alone; the new bend must be positioned one-third of the way along the shank, measured from the eye, and you must ensure the hookpoint is angled directly towards the eye.

Once we had worked out the mechanics of the bent-hook, Bill and I then had to determine how, and where, to mount the bait on it for optimum results when tench fishing. Some anglers consider that scaled-down carp tackle and rigs are perfect for tench; however, tench are not just smaller versions of *Cyprinus carpio*, and it is vital to appreciate the fact that tench and carp feed differently – for example tench feed far more delicately, perhaps partly because of their lack of bulk. Therefore subtle 'tuning' of a proven carp rig is required in order to make it more effective when tench are the target.

Our ideas would incorporate the bristle-rig method of attaching the bait to the hair. This clever yet amazingly simple idea of Bill's is a real time-saver since it does away with baiting needles, and fiddly bits of plastic as bait stops. The most critical problem to consider, however, is relative to the hook if consistent success with shy-feeding tench is to be enjoyed. Most diagrams depicting the bent-hook rig show the bait positioned close to the hook's eye; my own experience, however, leads me to believe that when tench are sought, it is better to position the bait at the back of the hook, and adjacent to the original bend. It is my firm conviction that anglers who haven't enjoyed success with the bent-hook rig have not given sufficient consideration to bait position.

Some maintain that the bent-hook rig is effective *only* in conjunction with pop-up baits; however when tench fishing, this is not true.

There is another exception to normal tench-fishing practice when using the bent-hook rig: the long hooklinks usually so necessary to fool shy-biting tench, should not be employed. To exploit this rig to the full, hooklinks should be no longer than 4in (100mm) and half this distance can often prove even more effective. As it is important to understand what is going on underwater, I will try to explain why this should be so.

To check a bait for resistance, and hence possible danger, a tench moves cautiously. Nevertheless, its initial movement is most likely to be its most fervent. Use of a very short hooklink, in conjunction with a heavyish bomb, increases the chances of the tench pricking itself on the hook. Furthermore, these days it is almost standard practice to employ long hooklinks for tench, which have therefore become accustomed to not experiencing tackle resistance until they have moved some distance with the bait. A short hooklink may be just enough to confuse them.

Just one final point: after considerable success with carp last summer (1990), next season's tench campaign will find me using the Drennan company's commercial variant of the bristle – the Boilie-Bayonet. This, coupled with the same company's unique hook concept, the Starpoint, could further enhance the effectiveness of the bent-hook rig. I sincerely hope so!

13

SYWELL

Mike Davison

There can be little doubt that at the moment, Northamptonshire's Sywell Reservoir is one of the most productive big tench waters in the country. The absolute maximum size of fish may be well short of many southern gravel pits, but for sheer numbers of six-, seven- and eight-pounders it probably cannot be beaten. Recently there has even been a sprinkling of nine-pounders.

The reservoir was originally constructed by a local water company, but long ago became redundant as far as its original purpose was concerned; in fact a few years ago there was serious talk of filling it in with rubbish. Fortunately this ridiculous idea was dropped and the reservoir and surrounding area has become a country park, used not just by anglers but by thousands of other people as well, who just want to relax.

The dam was constructed below the junction of two streams and it therefore formed a Y-shaped water. The total area is around 80 acres, and the depth follows the typical pattern of the deepest water at the dam end and the two arms shelving up to almost nothing at the stream inlets. There is a prolific growth of weed all around the edges and this leads to many problems when it comes to fishing. The water is relatively clean and clear – perhaps less so than the typical southern big tench pits – though strangely, it does not seem to be very rich. Where a handful of weed dragged from a typical estate lake in Norfolk would be teeming with life, a similar handful from Sywell is likely to contain no animal life at all. Despite this, tench at Sywell have always grown big; in the 1960s for example, when five- and six-pounders were rare, Sywell produced lots of them. Since then the tench fishing declined, but now the cycle seems to have come round again and the fish are bigger than ever.

So what makes Sywell such an exceptional tench water? It seems to me that two important factors are the lack of competition, and paradoxically, the scarcity of successful spawning conditions. Normally one would expect the weight distribution of fish, including tench, to follow the typical pyramid distribution. In other words there should be fish of all weights, but with smaller ones the most common, becoming progressively rare with increasing size, with just a few whoppers at the top of the pyramid. At Sywell we have lots of fish mostly of a similar size, and it appears that the vast majority of the tench currently being caught originate from the 1976 spawning season. Spawning can be observed every season, but it seems that the survival rate is normally very low. Of course the scorching spring and summer of 1976 resulted in successful spawning all over the country, but I am told that at Sywell there was an additional plus factor in that the water level dropped to expose much of the shallows. When the level rose again these areas were enriched, and an abundance of food and cover was available for the newly hatched fry. It certainly seems to be the case that in 1976 existing adult tench stocks were very low, and that for whatever reason the spawning and survival rate in that year was very high; and it is these fish which are forming the large catches of today.

Following their good start in life, these tench have had little competition for the available food and have continued to thrive. There are reasonable stocks of roach and rudd, but the tench have no other competition.

If these factors explain why there are so many big tench in the reservoir at present, they also unfortunately mean that the situation will not last much longer. If the fish are now fourteen years old they should be at or very near to their limit of growth. Weights in June 1990 were well up on previous years, but this seems to be due to the fact that fish were carrying rather more spawn than is normal for the water. A very warm spell early in the spring probably meant that they began to produce spawn early. Certainly females caught at the start of the season were noticeably more plump than usual – normally one has to look twice to see if a Sywell tench is carrying spawn.

Although the above factors may explain why the water has more recently produced so many big tench, it does not explain why those in the current batch have grown considerably larger than in the past. High protein baits are now extensively used, but this has only been the case for the past few years. The fish were certainly already exhibiting exceptional growth before these baits were used widely. Personally I doubt whether even now bait is an important factor for the population as a whole. There are an awful lot of tench and after the first few weeks of the season angling pressure drops considerably. The most likely reason for the improved growth rates is therefore intensification of agricultural methods and enrichment of the water due to run-off of fertilisers and so on; though only time will tell if this is the case. If it is, then perhaps when the cycle is repeated and the next successful generation of tench comes along, they will be bigger than ever.

Much of the approach to fishing at Sywell is dictated by various rules and restrictions imposed first by the controlling club, and also by the county council which runs the country park. Each will maintain that the rules are simply to satisfy the other, and I accept that an attempt has to be made to reconcile the conflicting demands of all users, be they humans or wildlife. It is up to the angler, therefore, to meet the challenge and catch within the rules and restrictions. In fact although they might seem a bit of a bind at times, I think that at Sywell they do give everyone an even chance, and have probably increased my own catches.

What are the restrictions? Well, the first is that the bulk of the two shallow arms are designated as nature reserves and are therefore closed to anglers. This is fair enough, but of course it is in these shallow areas that the tench congregate at spawning time – before these were closed to fishermen they were the most popular and productive in the early season and it is not surprising that the best early season swims are those closest to these areas.

The second restriction is that no night fishing is allowed: the angler and all his gear must be off the water by dusk. This means that there is no guarantee of getting the same swim two days running; conversely it also prevents people occupying the better swims for weeks on end, so everyone has a chance to fish them.

In the past anglers spent many hours, even days, clearing swims with a weed drag before fishing. Now, of course, nobody bothers to do this because there is no guarantee of fishing the swim the next day, or indeed ever again. A few hardy souls have taken to fishing some swims wearing their swimming trunks; as soon as they hit a fish they grab the landing net and go in after it! Anglers must consider their conscience when fishing such weedy swims: if they are losing a large proportion of fish in the weed and can't sort the matter out, they should move on.

The no-night-fishing rule obviously also rules out any pre-baiting, as you may not be able to fish the swim you have baited. It also makes it very difficult to try and work out any patrol routes or feeding patterns, if they exist, again because you may be fishing different swims every time you fish.

The eastern arm is smaller than the western and is partly overgrown with reed, so the western arm is therefore most popular at the start of the season, even though it means a long walk to the southern side of the arm, or a very long walk to the north. The eastern side of the reservoir is also very productive, and often produces more than the arms as the season draws on. Having said this, there is probably not a swim on the whole water which will not produce tench: basically if you can find a hole in the weed or cast past it you can catch a tench, eventually.

For the first few days of the season the anglers who head for the south side of the west arm have come to a gentleman's agreement to draw lots for the choice of swim, and to rotate on subsequent days so that the same angler does not fish the same swim twice. This gives everyone an even chance, and avoids multiple heart attacks as we all sprint towards the end peg laden with a mountain of gear. This season (1990) I was lucky enough to get first pick on 16 June and fished the best swim, the end one. It more than lived up to my expectations and my opening day catch included three eight-pounders, one of these a new personal best at 8lb 13oz. The following day I drew peg 5, a swim on a small promontory. Although quite a promising-looking swim I had never done very well here, and indeed had blanked on the previous 16 June.

I've tried to cut down on the gear but I still take too much, and the climb up the dam wall seems to get longer and harder every time. By the time I reached the swim I was shattered and all I really wanted to do was get my breath back, cool down and get the kettle on. However, the objective was to catch some tench. The sun was still too low for its rays to penetrate the glassy surface of the water, so it was impossible to pick out weedbeds; anyway, it would take a while to search the swim thoroughly by casting a bomb about, so that could wait until the light was good enough to do the job properly. Given the high numbers of tench there was a good chance there would be some in front of me – it is often possible to pull out a fish or two right away if disturbance is kept to a minimum. My rods were carried with the rigs ready assembled, and all I had to do was clip on the bombs and make just a couple of casts to find spots which seemed weed-free. Then each was cast out with a few boilies on a PVA stringer.

Before I had even finished unpacking the rest of my gear, one of the baits was taken and the monkey began to rise and fall steadily on its needle. The quick-start tactic had worked again. I picked up the rod and wound down; there was a satisfying thump from the other end of the line and the rod arched round. The fish made several short powerful runs – I made no attempt to stop them because I knew that while it stayed in open water I could stay in charge. A light carp rod and 8lb line soon got the better of the fish and I started to regain line. I hadn't fully explored the swim, but I knew I would have to bring it through a band of weed if it was to grace the net. Sure enough, as soon as the tench caught sight of cover it gave a few flicks of its paddle-like tail and plunged deep into the lush green sanctuary. Everything went solid. I couldn't tell whether the fish was still on, or if it had left the bomb wedged in the roots and fled.

I walked along the bank to my right so that I could pull from a different angle; all I could feel was the line grating against the stalks. I repeated the exercise to my left, but there was still no movement. There was only one thing left to try. I returned to the swim, slackened off and opened the bail arm. It began to look as if the fish had gone. Then after what seemed like an age, the line began to cut steadily through the water. The fish had freed itself. I snapped shut the bail arm and recommenced the fight. The runs were less powerful now, and this time when the fish came to the weed it collected no more than some over its nose and then allowed itself to be guided straight in with only a few token waves of the tail. As it was drawn slowly over the waiting net there were still few clues as to its size because it was engulfed in a ball of shiny green vegetation and it was impossible to tell how much was weed and how much tench.

However, as I lifted the net I could tell that it was a decent fish. I lay the net on the grass and carefully pulled aside the weed. It was obviously well over 8lb, and probably nearly as big as the one I had caught the day before. As I prepared the weighing gear my companion John Issitt predicted that the fish would be a new personal best. And when I lifted the Avons I could hardly believe what they told me, so without reading the figure out loud I asked him to check the weight with his own scales. They gave me the same figure, 9lb 2oz.

The fish was put in a sack to wait until there was enough light for a good photograph, and although I was now too elated to care very much what happened for the rest of the day, I carried on with the normal routine. A more thorough exploration of the swim was carried out and two areas baited up. There were definitely tench there, so a hundred boilies were placed in each, and a few more in diagonal lines extending from the main areas in the hope that fish patrolling closer in or further out would be intercepted and drawn to the baited areas. The rods were re-cast, this time having inserted foam into one of the double baits to achieve a neutral buoyancy with one bait balanced on top of the other. Normally tench are very inquisitive, as well as greedy, so a double mouthful is quite likely to be taken from amongst a carpet of single baits. The neutral buoyancy ensures that the bait will not sink into weed or silt

Mike Davison looks well pleased with this 9lb 2oz Sywell chunk

and be hidden, as well as making it behave more naturally when picked up.

The baits were placed on a very short hair, almost touching the size 8 hook. About 2 feet of multi-strand hook-length linked the hook to a semi-fixed 1¾oz bomb; semi-fixed leads seem to be the most effective, but they must be used in conjunction with a heavy monkey. Indication of drop-back runs is always a problem, and also the fact that your line is likely to be draped through weed. Some people have resorted to line heavier than 8lb, but I take the view that if you need stronger gear than that, it's because you are trying to winch the fish in weed and all, and as this can cause unacceptable damage to the fish I would rather move swims.

Boilies certainly seem to have become the most popular and successful bait, but the mix seems to be relatively unimportant. I always use strongly flavoured and sweetened baits for tench, though others have done well with fishy flavours. Rather surprisingly, Sywell tench do not seem to have become wary of bright colours.

Although on that occasion I was using fixed leads, there is no need to stick rigidly to the same method all the time; any approach can be successful on the right day. One of my own best catches (eighteen fish for 108lb) was taken almost entirely using mini-boilies, 6lb line, Avon rod and a tiny bobbin indicator. By hitting the bites rather than fishing the bolt I was generally able to turn the fish before they reached the weed. I wouldn't expect to get away with this later in the year when the weed is thicker, but it is certainly worth considering. With standard bolt rigs the fish

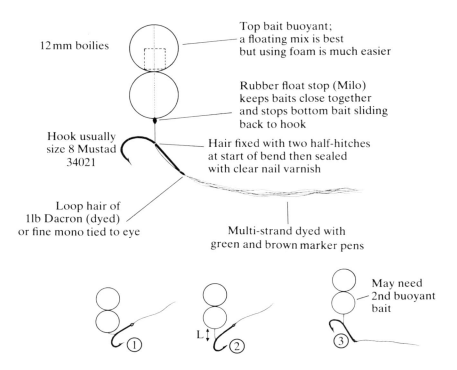

12 mm boilies

Top bait buoyant;
a floating mix is best
but using foam is much easier

Rubber float stop (Milo)
keeps baits close together
and stops bottom bait sliding
back to hook

Hook usually
size 8 Mustad
34021

Hair fixed with two half-hitches
at start of bend then sealed
with clear nail varnish

Loop hair of
1lb Dacron (dyed)
or fine mono tied to eye

Multi-strand dyed with
green and brown marker pens

May need
2nd buoyant
bait

Depending on how buoyant top bait is three different presentations
are possible without any other changes to rig.

① 2nd bait rests on lake bed with 1st (buoyant) bait balanced
on top of it

② Both baits float above lake bed. Distance determined by
length of hair (L)

③ Rig balanced so that the hook just rests on the lake
bed with its point lifted off the bottom. This is easier
to achieve with a heavy hook such as the Mustad 34021

Diagram 44 Mike Davison's double boilie pop-up rig

is travelling at full pelt and is often already weeded by the time you pick up the rod.

Although there were obviously fish in the swim I didn't get another take for an
hour and a half. This one weighed 7lb 2oz. I topped up each area with another ten
baits, as I do following every run or if fish are seen rolling; and if I think there are a
lot of fish present, this rate may be increased. The swim would also be topped up
with fresh bait in the early evening, even if there had been little action.

For my purposes, relatively heavy baiting with strongly flavoured bait is appro-
priate; remember that anglers at Sywell are fishing different swims all the time, so it

is not a case of training fish to expect bait in a certain place at a regular time. A lot of tench may pass through the swim during the course of the day, and the object is to stop them in their tracks. On the other hand if the fish don't show up, there is no point in continuing to pile it in.

A little before 8am the light had improved, so the first fish could be photographed and returned. I had just watched it swim away and was wiping the tape measure clean when one of the monkeys began to dance. I threw the tape to the ground and grabbed the rod, and this time the fight went my way. The fish lunged repeatedly for the weedbeds but I managed to prevent it becoming badly snagged. By now I had a better mental picture of the bottom and knew the areas to avoid. When it reached the clear shallows I caught occasional glances of a huge emerald flank: this was one that must *not* get away! There was little danger now that the fish would pass through the weed, so I slackened off the clutch and allowed it to make a few short runs. When I sensed it was ready, I stepped up the pressure and eased it over the rim of the waiting net without a hitch.

Longer than the first fish, it looked even bigger, but the needle on the scales stopped at exactly 9lb. A day earlier I had thought that a nine-pounder was probably an impossibility. Having seen the extra spawn that the fish taken on opening day had been carrying, we had agreed that somebody somewhere would catch one. Now in a morning I had caught two myself. Rather like winning the pools, then being told that your premium bond has come up as well!

The second '9' of the day – this one 9lb exactly – proving that dreams can come true

POSTSCRIPT

When the idea for this book was originally put together, I was expecting and even courting a measure of controversy. After all, when you assemble a team of highly successful and individual anglers such as have contributed within these pages, you might expect some diversity and even outright contradiction. Therefore when the manuscripts came in, I was more than a little surprised to find that rather than oppose each other, the general tendency was for each chapter to broaden the various subjects covered. In fact, in the main, they all tended to pull together in a rather complementary way!

Of course there are different ideas and approaches expressed, but it seems to me that generally they work well together and enrich the subject of tench fishing. Certainly, some of the contributions have given me some food for thought, and my good friend John Bailey openly admitted that the manuscript had given him many ideas for the new season. And when you think about it, to offer a few ideas is as much as one could ask from any fishing book, other than being a good read. So all there remains for me to say, is that I hope *Success with Big Tench* will have given you, the reader, a variety of ideas to work into your own fishing. Should this result in singing lines, wet sacks and perhaps even that excellent feeling one has when the camera shutter opens on a fish, the size of which was once just a dream, then no-one will be happier than me!

ACKNOWLEDGEMENTS

My sincere thanks are offered, first of all, to Mr Friend, who is now long departed. It was he who took the time, during the summer of 1960, to sit patiently beside me on the bank and tutored me through the capture of my very first tench. My thanks also go to all those who contributed to this book, to John Bailey for editing the text, to Margrette Sadd and Binsie Rumsey for help with word processing, and last but not least to Jim Bigden and Simon Lush, not only for allowing me to use their photographs, but also for being partners through some of the best tenching one could ask for.

INDEX

INDEX